...tting and Time Management

By
Louise Tondeur

www.emer

70001493765 8

Emerald Publishing

© Copyright Dr Louise Tondeur 2012

ISBN: 9781847162731

Author Photograph by Sarah Barnsley
Cover Design by Bookworks Islington

Contents

Part 1: Goal setting

Part 1: Goal setting

Chapter 1: Small Steps to Goal Setting

Small steps in a nutshell

You can take a task, however daunting, and break it down into smaller and smaller steps until it becomes manageable. You can do small things in your everyday life to allow you to achieve what you want to.

About this chapter

This chapter introduces the small steps method. I start by telling you more about how this book works. Then I'll ask you to begin to think about yourself and your aspirations and show you the ten small steps principles. The rest of the chapter includes the basics of keeping a journal, and a definition of what a goal *is* and what a goal *isn't*. It finishes with a brief introduction to Abraham Maslow's *hierarchy of needs* and some practical exercises for you to try.

Small steps to goal setting: an introduction
About this book.
This book is designed to do four things:
- You'll be introduced to the small steps method.
- You'll learn how to set personal, value-led goals.
- You'll learn the principles of time management.
- You're given a list of resources, as well as access to the Small Steps Method website, to help you take things further.

The book is divided into two halves: goal-setting and time management. This introduction gives you the basic overview of the small steps method. Both sections of the book elaborate on it. The advice in the first section is designed to fit any kind of goal-setting, whether it relates to a personal ambition, your career, a charity or business, or a group of people with a shared dream.

Discovering your goals: An overview of you.

First I'd like to invite you to do an overview of you. Right now, whatever you are doing with your life, what's good about being you? Take a moment to appreciate yourself. What are your dreams and ambitions and your hopes for the future? Is there anything you'd like to change? Are there any skills you'd like to develop?

The small steps method

The small steps method is about taking a task – any task – and breaking it down into small steps. It doesn't matter what that task is, the same principles apply. Here are the small step principles, in a nutshell, followed by an example. This is the first time I've articulated them, especially for this book. The rest of the book is dedicated to showing you how to apply the small steps method to goal setting and time management.

1. Small steps are small. Break down a task until you get to something you could easily achieve today.

2. Small steps are specific and concrete. Make the small steps as down-to-earth and measurable as possible, if it suits you.

3. Small steps don't cost a fortune. Do as many free steps as possible first. Financing a project can also be broken down into small steps.

4. Small steps are just like footsteps: Take one small step and take another small step after it. Keep taking small steps.

5. Small steps are just small steps. They don't rely on luck, on other people, or on results.

6. Small steps don't necessarily go in a straight line. One action doesn't have to lead directly to the next, as long as they all relate back to the task.
7. Take lots of small steps, especially at the beginning.
8. Turn up. Small steps require you to get off the sofa.
9. Once you've prepared, you can do small steps without even thinking about it.
10. Small steps deserve to be appreciated. Pause at regular intervals to acknowledge your progress and to keep in check. Keep some kind of record in a notebook or journal, on a computer or on your blog.

What you need to do to understand and follow the small steps method:

Throughout this book, I suggest that you do some exercises. This is a common theme of the small steps method – small practical exercises that:

- Help you to be more aware of your life, your values and your goals.
- Help you to practice a technique or idea.

Do the exercises in a notebook or on your computer or hand-held device. This will form a record of your progress. The exercises are all optional. In fact, they won't all be relevant or attractive to you. Pick those you're interested in. Leave the others. I suggest that you do these exercises in a notebook (paper or digital) *so that you can collect them in one place and look back over them.* You might want separate notebooks for some of the other suggestions, like the bugs diary (in chapter twelve) or the food diary (in chapter thirteen), if you choose to do them. The notebooks are specifically for jotting down the results of the exercises in this book. Often I ask you to carry one around, so you may want to buy a portable one! By the way, some of the exercises are repeated, getting more advanced or more detailed each time. This is deliberate: so that you're introduced to a concept first and then given time to work on it.

Keeping a journal
What is a journal?
You may find it helpful to keep a journal while you are working towards particular goals. This particularly relates to small steps principle number 10. A journal is a place to record a commentary on the process. It's also a place to record your thoughts and feelings, dreams and ideas. You can use it like a scrapbook too. Where an exercise asks you to think about your thoughts and feelings about a particular issue, you could include this in your journal. Again, this is optional. You might feel that the more straightforward notebook is enough for you, although there are various reasons to keep a journal:

- Record it. Some people like to have a record of their progress in one particular goal or project. This kind of journal focuses on challenges and set backs, successes and unexpected pleasures resulting from the journey you've decided to undertake. For example, in chapter twelve I ask you to imagine a fictional person called Martin who wants to build his own house. He might want to record his progress like this.

- Practical ideas and suggestions. For his kind of project, Martin might need a place to set down practical details as he goes forward.

- Inspiration. You can also use a journal for inspirational images, words and snippets of text to help you to visualise where you want to go.
- Get it out. You can use a journal for self-expression - to vent in whatever way you want to.

Using your journal to complete your plan.
Chapter three includes a number of goal setting activities. Once you've worked through them you'll have a complete list of the goals you want to achieve. If you decide to use a journal, you can include a goal plan at the beginning.

Who writes about journaling?
If you're interested in journaling and want to take it further, you might find the following writers useful.

- Julia Cameron suggests keeping Morning Pages in the bestselling *The Artist's Way* and *The Sound of Paper*. You can also find out more on her website. Have a look at the resources section.
- Therapeutic writing. It's beyond the scope of this book but you can find lots of information on journaling in books on therapeutic writing. There are some suggestions in the resources section.

What is a goal?
Defining 'a goal'
Before you start setting goals, it's useful to figure out exactly what a goal is:

- concrete and specific (or at least can be turned this way). You will never know if a goal is achievable - or *even something you actually want to do* – unless you make it concrete and specific. Concrete means you'll know if you've achieved it. It's something you could actually do in real terms. Specific means getting down to the nitty-gritty of what you would have to do to achieve the goal. It's not general or vague. If you find yourself feeling a little suspicious or cynical about specific and measurable goals, have a look at chapter seven now: I review Stephen M. Shapiro's 'goal-free' approach there.

- something you want to achieve. It's odd when you think about it but a lot of us go round with (usually rather vague and non-specific) goals that come from what other people expect of us, or that we have heard somewhere are good ideas. Let go of it if you don't really want to do it.

- a goal is attached to a reason (even if it's 'because I fancy it'). One danger with goal setting is that we make up goals to do with something we're not really interested in, just because it's become a habit. A goal has a reason attached to it – you know why you want to do it.

- a goal is often time-limited (or at least can be turned this way). Many writers on goal-setting agree that we need to be able to tell whether we've achieved a goal or not by using a timeframe. This is scary because it means committing to do something by a particular date, which is why many of our goals remain unformed in our heads and we never let go of those we don't really want to do. However, not all goal-setting gurus agree: for other approaches to goal setting, have a look at chapter seven.

- a goal is achievable (but it can be a challenge). This seems obvious at first sight but it's the chief paradox of goal-setting advice. Many writers tell us to dream big or even to dream the impossible. Some even seem to tell us that we don't need to take any action – just thinking about it enough will make it happen. A goal needs to be challenging *and* achievable.

And now, just to make sure, let's look at what a goal *isn't*:

- What you think you *should* do. A goal isn't guilt-laden; a goal is about what you *want* to achieve: sometimes a subtle difference, sometimes a huge one.
- What other people think you *should* do: it's impossible to dispel other people's expectations entirely – especially when they are close friends or relatives – but your heart will never be in it if you follow society's agenda or your parent's or next door neighbour's. Make sure they are *your* goals.
- What you *could* do: perhaps you *could* train to cross the Sahara Desert, win a pie eating contest, hike in the Andes – but do you want to? Idiomatic goals (used in the media as short-hand for high achievement) like writing a novel, running a marathon, swimming the Amazon and climbing Kilimanjaro can catch us out – it's ok if you don't.
- Inflexible or set in stone: a myth put about in some goal-setting self-help books is that we must do anything and everything to strive towards our goals. Not true! They might change. You might change.
- A promise or a guilt trip. You can change your mind; if you don't achieve your goal you've learnt something along the way.

Do you need a goal?

Bear in mind the results of the following exercise when considering whether you need to set a goal or goals in a part of your life:

1. Spend some time making a list of the skills you have – not only those you are paid for. Now make a list of skills you would like to improve. Refer back to this list as you work through the rest of this chapter. We'll return to this list again in chapter six.

2. Write these headings in your notebook: health, career, study, family, finances, travel, leisure, social. Do any of these stand out as particularly significant?

Aspirations and dreams v. what I need right now.
There are two kinds of goals. Seemingly impossible dreams on the one hand and the perhaps more mundane or everyday things I need to change right now. Aspirations and dreams are expressed as if they are way off in the future whereas 'things I need now' goals seem so immediate they can be overwhelming. You'll probably have *both* kinds of goals.

Shared goals.
Many goals are not individual ones. You may have the same goals as work colleagues or your life partner. Equally your goals might conflict. Even when a goal is an individual one it will still have an impact on others. Make an effort to understand any shared or conflicting goals. Do your research so you know what you're talking about.

Overlapping goals.
Goals generate other goals. Some goals automatically generate *overlapping* goals: goals I need to achieve at the same time. For example: 'I want to start a family' not only has an impact on others, it brings financial goals with it, which might generate career goals: perhaps 'I want a steady job' or 'I want to work freelance.' It also generates overlapping health goals. For example: 'I'm going to give up alcohol.'

Overlapping and overwhelming?

Overlapping goals can feel overwhelming. Deal with them by breaking each one down into small steps. Then take small steps towards each goal every week. I recently found the notebook where we planned small steps towards achieving our goal of having a family. Seeing it brought back all those overwhelming feelings about the prospect of going through IVF, the cost, emotional and financial, the thought of having to lose weight and get fit, the idea of having to inject myself! The *only way* I could do it was by breaking it down into manageable steps. Then I looked at my son and realised we'd done it! It didn't matter about those difficult feelings – we did it anyway. You know what? Even if it hadn't worked I would still be glad that I had tried. By the way, I also discovered we had written 'Build our own house' - something we haven't done yet – and it generated those same overwhelming feelings about cost, difficulty and expectations.

Separate goals.

Once you break down a goal into steps, it might generate completely separate goals: goals I need to achieve first. For example, if you needed to do another qualification before enrolling on a college course or if you needed to boost your confidence before applying for a volunteer position. Separate goals are easier than overlapping goals because you can manage them one at a time, but they can be frustrating because you can feel as though they are holding you back.

When you realise you have a set of separate goals, it helps to work out a medium-term timeframe for yourself: *I will have achieved my goal in X number of years.* Doing so also allows you to note any time constraints. Time constraints can turn separate goals into overlapping goals.

Your hierarchy of needs

In the 1940s, psychologist Abraham Maslow expressed all the things human beings need as a hierarchy, called the *hierarchy of needs*. It's usually drawn as a pyramid, and has five levels. At the bottom are physiological or biological needs, followed by safety, love / belonging and esteem, with self-actualisation at the top. Maslow argued that each level of need must be satisfied before those above it, and so on, up the hierarchy. Without fulfilling our basic needs – having enough food to eat or a safe place to live - we can't look after our 'higher' needs that might include achieving our goals. Another way of putting this is that we all have physical, psychological / emotional, social, cultural and spiritual needs. To neglect one kind of need will impact on the other.

Food chain

For example, food is a physiological need – on the bottom rung of Maslow's *Hierarchy*. Do you eat breakfast? Do you keep your blood sugar level balanced? Do you eat enough fruit and veg? All of these things affect our mental health and our physical health, and therefore have an impact on how we manage our daily routine. Long term they create a chain reaction and have an impact on whether we achieve our goals or whether achieving our goals makes us happy. Following Maslow's idea of a hierarchy, it would be foolish to neglect healthy eating because we're chasing a deadline or under pressure in another area of our lives. I'm talking to myself as much as to anyone else here but if you think about it, it also doesn't make sense to argue that we *don't have enough time* to eat healthily.

Initial exercises
The many parts of your life.

Take a moment now to stop and think about the many parts of your life. It helps to begin thinking this way because it's a theme that we'll return to later. Is there anything you'd like to add? Any life part that's missing? We'll come back to this at the beginning of chapter three.

Things I must do before I'm / Things I've always wanted to do but...

At the back of most of our minds is the idea that we'll do X before we reach a certain age or before we get married or before we have children. Most of us also have a vague idea of things we've always wanted to do and a 'but' stopping us from doing them. Taking time to write them down begins to make them concrete so we can either let them go, or take action. Make a note of yours.

Small steps practice

Try the following three-part exercise:

1. Flowchart. In your notebook, create the boxes for a flowchart. Now chart the steps you need to drink a glass of water. Be as specific as possible.
2. Picture. This time *draw* the steps you need to take to drink a glass of water.
3. Write it. Now *write down* the small steps.

Small ways to keep check

If you do the practical exercises step-by-step as you work through this book you'll automatically be keeping a check on your progress. Here are some other ways to keep on top:

- A Grateful List. Stop for a moment, whenever you can, and make a list of things you are grateful for right now. This is a real mood lifter and helps to put our goals in perspective.
- Review your small steps once a day - on the train to work, for instance - and incorporate them into your daily routine somehow.

- Alternatively, review your small steps once a week and add them to a schedule for the rest of the week. Every Monday evening, for instance.
- Chat with any other people involved at least once a week. If others are directly involved in your project, schedule meetings at work or at home as appropriate. Good communication is vital.

One of the closing chapters of this book takes you through other small ways you can keep in check.

Key points
In this chapter we've covered:
1. The ten small steps principles
2. An overview of you
3. Keeping a journal
4. Defining 'a goal': you don't have to write a novel, run a marathon, swim the Amazon and climb Kilimanjaro if you don't want to.
5. Life parts: health, career, study, family, finances, travel, leisure, social.
6. Understanding shared or conflicting goals
7. Overlapping goals: goals I need to achieve at the same time.
8. Separate goals: goals I need to achieve first.
9. Your hierarchy of needs
10. Initial exercises and small ways to keep in check

****

Chapter 2: The Small-Steps Method in Action

About this chapter
This chapter gives you an example of the small steps method in action, followed by some mind loosening exercises designed to get you used to *divergent* rather than *convergent* thinking.

Rhonda, the wannabe radio journalist
Rhonda
Here's the goal-setting example that uses the small steps method. It's about a prospective radio journalist: let's call her Rhonda. You may have no interest in radio journalism. Bear with me. It's an example of the small steps method in action. Rhonda's goal is to become a radio journalist.

If you were Rhonda, the wannabe radio journalist, what small steps might you take?

- Write down your goal and make it specific: *By the time I am 35, I have a regular slot as a sports reporter on a major radio station.*
- Use the internet to research routes into your chosen career.
- Go to the local library to browse their careers resources.
- Find out about local colleges in your area.
- Download more information about journalism courses.
- Attend an open evening.
- Fill in an application form.

- Look up local hospitals online to see if they have a radio station.
- Email three hospital radio stations.
- Post a request for contacts on a social media network.

What happens next?

While studying journalism at college, Rhonda volunteers at a hospital radio once a fortnight. She meets someone there who invites her to do work experience at a local radio station. While doing work experience, she meets someone who works as a sports reporter. He gives Rhonda advice about how to approach potential employers. She sends a sample of her slot on the hospital radio show to a friend of a weak contact. One of the people she's contacted so far emails to tell her about a job as a stand-in traffic reporter. She gets the job as the stand-in traffic reporter and....

The small steps method in action:

- All of these small steps can be set in motion in a few minutes or a few hours.
- All of the steps are specific, measurable, down-to-earth and concrete.
- All of these initial steps can be done for free.
- All of these steps simply require you to identify and complete the next small step *even if it seems as though nothing much is happening.*
- None of these steps happen through luck. While 'meeting someone who works as a sports reporter' might seem like luck, just as you're more likely to get on a bus if you stand at a bus stop, you're more likely to meet a sports broadcaster if you're at a radio station!

- Although she's supported and advised by other people, each step requires her to be proactive herself.
- She doesn't wait for one of the steps to yield results before trying another small step. This is a common stumbling block and important for goal setting, especially in the initial stages.
- You'll notice that one step doesn't necessarily lead to the next but it always relates back to the original goal.
- Although each step is small, our prospective radio journalist goes for multiple approaches to her goal at first: research, a college course, volunteering, work experience, asking for contacts.
- All of the steps require some action: they require her to turn up.
- She's clearly thought carefully about how to achieve her goal and broken it down into small steps. After that, some steps she can just do without thinking about it too much – like turning up at the library or the open evening or emailing the radio stations – to avoid analysis paralysis.
- We don't know if she pauses at regular intervals to appreciate her progress or whether she keeps a record. We *can* tell, however, that the whole process will work much better if she does do these things. Far from being too touchy-feely, this level of awareness will have a real impact on whether she achieves her goal.
- While 'become a radio journalist' might seem impossible, now it's broken down into very specific steps it feels achievable.

Mind loosening exercises

Why do these exercises?

These exercises are designed to enable to you to think *divergent* thoughts about goal-setting rather than *convergent* thoughts – more on that later. Do them even if they feel silly, strange or impossible, that's a sign that you're thinking differently.

Mind loosening exercise number 1. Life parts.

1. Choose **one** part of your life to focus on from: health, career, study, family, finances, travel, leisure, social. Write it as a heading in your notebook.
2. Write down one thing you want to achieve in that part of your life. Do a quick check: if you had done this thing, how would you feel? Can you visualise yourself completing it? Is this something you want to achieve in 1 year, 5 years, 10 years or 20 years? Rewrite the goal to make it as concrete and specific as possible.
3. Make a list of any actions related to the goal that:
   a. can be done in 5 mins.
   b. can be done in half an hour.
   c. can be done in a day.
4. Look back over your notes. Why haven't you done the things on your list already? Be honest. It will help you to discover blocks and also whether you genuinely want to achieve the goal.

Mind loosening exercise number 2: Draw pictures.

1. Pick one of following areas of your life: health, career, study, family, finances, travel, leisure, social. Draw an image representing what it looks like now and what it will look like in the future. Take your time, but you don't need to be a great artist for this to work.
2. Use colour. Make the images as big and bold as possible.

3. Give each picture a caption.
4. Review what you've done by writing some notes in your notebook.

Mind loosening exercise number 3: Trip to Europa.

1. Scientists think there could be life on one of Jupiter's moons: under the frozen sea that covers Europa. You're going to plan a trip there!

2. Draw a flowchart. On one side of the paper draw a box and inside the box write your goal as *if you have already achieved it*, in the present tense. For example: 'I am swimming in the oceans of Europa.'

3. Work back across the paper, drawing boxes to represent each step you would need to take to achieve this goal. Any blank boxes represent gaps in your knowledge that will become a research plan.

4. Create a list of gaps in your knowledge using the blank boxes as a guide. Turn this into a research plan.

5. Review what you've done in your notebook. You're probably not going to achieve this goal or carry out the research, unless you work for Nasa! The aim of this activity is to practise working out the small steps you need to achieve *any* seemingly impossible goal.

Key points
In this chapter we've covered:

- Rhonda, the wanna-be radio journalist. An example of the small-steps method in action.
- Mind loosening exercises: *divergent* verses *convergent* thinking.

Chapter 3: Goal-Setting

About this chapter

This chapter takes you through several goal setting activities. Work through them in your notebook or journal and you'll end up with a complete list of goals you want to achieve. Once you've completed the exercises in this chapter you'll have generated lists of actions related to your goals – it's these actions that you'll be breaking down using the small steps method.

Goal setting exercises

Goal setting exercise number 1: My Goals

You're going to repeat the first mind loosening exercise from chapter two, but this time take longer over it. Start by creating your own *life parts*.

1. Divide your life into parts. First time round we used the generic subheadings of health, career, study, family, finances, travel, leisure, social. This time try to be more specific. Come up with as many life parts as possible by answering these questions.

    a) What do you do with your time? Don't evaluate. Just make a list. For example, I like cooking and I sing in a choir.

    b) What roles (or parts) do you play each day? For example, I'm a mother, a partner, a daughter, a teacher and a writer. Check that these life parts are all important to you.

2. Strike out any life parts where you know you don't want to set goals. For example, cooking is very important to me, but I don't have any cooking goals.

3. Decide on the most important part of your life *for goal setting* right now. Focus on one area at a time. Write it as a heading in your notebook.

4. Make a list of what you would like to achieve in this area of your life. Note any shared goals. Decide which are aspirations or big dreams and which are more everyday goals but just as important.

5. Visualise yourself achieving each goal. Take time to picture it in detail and to experience how you would feel. If this visualisation makes you feel excited or apprehensive or enthusiastic, this is a goal you're interested in. If it makes you feel uninspired or you can't be bothered to do this part of the exercise, strike this goal off your list – it's a 'should' or a 'could' and not a genuine goal.

6. *Even if it feels impossible*, set a time frame. When will you achieve each goal? Is this something you want to achieve in 6 months, 1 year, 5 years, 10 years or 20 years?

7. What would half-way look like? For example, if your goal is to be debt free in five years time, what will you have achieved in 2 and a half years?

8. Rewrite each goal to make it as concrete and specific as possible, if you like working this way.

9. Take one goal at a time. Make a list of any actions related to the goal that:
   a) can be done in 5 mins.
   b) can be done in half an hour.
   c) can be done in a day.

10. Look back over your notes. Why haven't you done the things on your list already? Be honest. It will help you to discover blocks and also whether you genuinely want to achieve the goal.

11. Repeat this process until you've recorded your goals for all the life parts you want to include.

12. Do a final check to make sure you are not setting goals for anything you're not interested in.

13. Select the goals you want to work on. If you've come up with a large number of goals, pick the ones you are *most* excited by and make sure you have a balance from different parts of your life. Some will be big dreams, some will be more everyday. Most goal-setting writers suggest that you don't have more than 7 or 8 at a time.

14. Repeat steps 12 and 13 in a week's time.

15. Make yourself a list of goals.

Goal setting exercise number 2: Charting your goals.

1. Review your notes so far.

2. Create a table on a computer or draw yourself a chart. A computerised version makes it easier to adjust. Give it six columns. **You can download a ready-made chart from the Small Steps website.**

3. Now add column headings for the goal, the life part related to the goal, the reason for your goal, the time limit, and how you will reward yourself. Also include a column for what the half-way point will look like.

4. Add all of the goals you've selected to your chart.

5. In your notebook, record any emotions attached: excited, daunted, bored, reluctance, eager.

6. Write down any overlapping goals and any new goals. Ask: *What do you need to achieve first or at the same time?* for each of your goals.

Goal setting exercise number 3: Think big.

This exercise is designed to expand your thinking. You don't need to know how you would achieve these big goals– just have fun with it.

1. Look over the chart you created during exercise 2.
2. Look at one goal. Use your imagination to make the goal bigger.
3. In your notebook, write down a bigger goal. Now get even bigger.
4. Keep going. Get as big as possible. Write down a bigger goal each time.
5. Note any emotions attached as before.
6. Repeat this exercise for all of the goals on your list.
7. This exercise is designed to trick your mind into daring to dream big, by revealing what you'd do if money, time and responsibilities were no object.
8. Come back down to earth and adjust your chart. Do you need to make any of your goals bigger?

Now we'll repeat and elaborate on the other mind loosening exercises from chapter two, again spending longer over them.

Goal setting exercise number 4: Get ready to play.

This is a playful way to think about your goals. If you thought colouring in was for pre-schoolers think again! If you don't usually work like this, try to put ideas about how you're wasting your time to one side or jot them down in a notebook first. Give yourself enough time to fill the paper you chose. Working on this activity with other people is enlightening, too!

1. Equipment. Find the largest piece of paper you can. Use a roll of paper you can cover the floor or table with if possible. Get some big coloured pens to use.

2. Play music. While you write and draw, play something uplifting. I recommend Mozart. Turn it up.

3. Draw pictures. Think about each part of your life. (You identified these in *Goal setting exercise number 1: My Goals*.) Draw two images for each one: how it looks now and how it will look in the future. Take time over it but it doesn't matter if it doesn't look right because you also get to label each picture with a caption. Be as messy as you like. Doodling is encouraged.

4. Use colour. Try to get through all the colours you have. Don't stick with one. Keep going until you have filled the paper with colourful images and words.

5. Review what you've done. Get your notebook and write some notes on what you wrote and drew. If you love what you've produced, keep it. Stick it on the wall or keep it safe somewhere. If it's all too silly, put it in the recycling. This is might seem like an obvious or petty suggestion but it's important advice: too often we feel as if a task isn't finished simply because we're holding onto some physical aspect of it.

Goal setting exercise number 4. Flowcharts.

If you're used to being creative, colourful and messy, this can feel mechanical but actually it's a very creative exercise, which allows you to work an idea through to its conclusion. It might also feel like a hard task to keep coming up with more steps: that's the point. Be as specific as possible each time. Most people who do this activity in one of my workshops come away realising that what had been a vague half-formed idea is actually achievable. They also soon discover whether they want to put in the effort necessary to achieve their goal – and whether it's really a goal at all. **You can download two example flowcharts from the Small Steps website.**

1. Equipment. Find the largest piece of paper you can: a roll of paper you can cover the floor or table with if possible. Get some big black or blue marker pens to use. (Hint: NOT the kind that smell bad. Our olfactory system has a real impact on our emotional memory.)

2. Draw a flowchart. Try to draw these flowcharts as neatly and methodically as you can. No doodling. EITHER: Start from where you are now and:

   a) Draw a box for each one of the things you're involved in right now on the left-hand side of the paper.

   b) Draw subsequent boxes across the page with a next step in each one.

   c) Make each step start with a verb. If it's still an unformed or vague idea, write it down anyway, but use 'research' as your verb. You're not committing yourself yet. You're still playing with possibilities.

   d) Write a possible next step in each new box. Don't try to evaluate at this stage, just write the steps down. For example, one the things you're involved in right now might be 'working as a teacher.' Write that in a box on the left hand-side. The first possible step could be 'research teaching abroad'. The step after 'research teaching abroad' might be 'go to careers show'.

   e) Of course each box may have a number of possible next steps, but draw one line of steps at a time, then go back and create another line of steps.

f) Someone wise once told me that if you continue on the path you're on, you'll get where you're going. Include that possibility in your diagram. Draw a line showing the path of least resistance or what you'll end up doing if you don't go in a new direction. *Very often this isn't a bad thing* but it helps us to make conscious decisions.

g) Above and below each step, create implication boxes. Look back at the example of the prospective radio journalist in chapter two. What implications would she have to consider? Financial ones, if she has to pay for the course and practical ones if she needs to find a course with childcare attached. *Evaluating* implications can put us off before we've even considered how a goal might work. Don't evaluate yet. Simply list the implications in boxes or bubbles above and below each step. For example 'research option to work abroad' might have an implication box that reads 'leaving family behind for a year.'

OR: Start from where you want to be and:

a) Draw a box for each one of the things you know you want to achieve within a certain time limit on the right-hand side of the page.

b) Write these as if they are true, in the present tense. For example, *I own and run my own vineyard in the South of England.*

c) Take a step back and draw a box for it. You might want to make a list of backwards steps in your notebook first to get them in the right order. For example, 'buy a vineyard' might seem like the next backwards step from 'own and run my own vineyard' but remember you said *run* as well. You'll need some specific setting up steps for your vineyard too.

d) Keep going until you get back to where you are now.

e) You can draw 'implications boxes' around the steps as appropriate. An obvious one in this example is financial. Doing your flowchart this way is harder and forces you to confront gaps in your knowledge, giving you very specific areas to research. Don't be afraid to leave empty boxes.

3. Give yourself multiple options. This is why you need a big piece of paper because now you are allowed to become more divergent! Use your imagination. Go in and add more options to some of the key boxes on the flowchart. Make them a different colour.

4. Have a time limit. Work in twenty-five minute bursts, with a five minute rest after each. (This is an example of Francesco Cirillo's Pomodoro Technique in action. Have a look in the resources section for more.) Do no more than three twenty-five minute bursts at a time.

5. Review what you've done. Get your notebook and write some notes on your flowchart. As with the drawing exercise, if you love the results, keep it. Stick it on the wall or keep it safe somewhere. If not, record what you need, then put it in the recycling.

To-do lists and master plans
Creating and using to-do lists

By the end of this section of the book, you'll have created a list of small steps relating to your goals. These will be specific actions that you'll then be encouraged to schedule in a morning, afternoon or evening slot, or to incorporate into your daily, weekly or monthly routine. You can handle these actions by keeping a Small Steps To-Do List. This can be as rough or as systematised as you like. A Small Steps To-Do List is a working document. Edit your list or lists as you complete some steps and add more. Either:

- keep one main Small Steps To-Do List containing all of your small steps. You can keep everyday tasks on this list too. Keeping one Small Steps To-Do List works well if you want to incorporate your goals into your daily life. OR:

- keep separate Small Steps To-Do Lists for each goal, perhaps in colour-coded box files, which you refer to when you've put aside time to work on a particular project. Your everyday to do list would also be separate, and probably stuck on the kitchen wall or somewhere very obvious. This works well if you want to keep your projects compartmentalised and in their specified time slots, but only if you allocate enough time to them. You can always add steps to your everyday list if and when you need to.

To-do list resources

- If you'd like a dynamic system for handling to do lists, have a look at Mark Forster's work. The latest is available for free from his website, which is listed in the resources section of this book.

- You might also like some of the suggestions in Ronni Eisenberg's book *Organise Yourself.*
- The Guardian recently included features on how to organise your life in their Saturday magazine. One article by Oliver Burkeman looked at digital solutions to organising your time, for example.

Master Plans

A Master Plan is a way of planning how to tackle a big goal that turns into a master to do list for that goal. You can do one for every goal you've set yourself or focus only on the most complicated or time-bound projects. There's more on Master Plans in Chapter 10. On the website you can download a guide to creating a Small Steps Master Plan. Do that now if you want to get started straightaway.

Key points

In this chapter we've covered several goal setting activities:

- In *my goals* you created your own list of life parts, set goals and a timeframe for each one, making the goals concrete and specific, and checking along the way that they're really *your* goals.
- In *charting your goals* you formalised the process by listing your goals in a chart with the timeframe and any emotions attached.
- In *thinking big* you used your chart to check if any of your goals need to get bigger.
- In *get ready to play* you tried drawing pictures, using colour and listening to music to release your creative side.
- In *creating flowcharts* you created small steps either starting from where you are now or from where you want to be. You

included implications and knowledge gaps and where you'll get to if you stay on the path you're on.

- In *to do lists and master plans* you began to think about how to organise your lists of small steps and I suggested some resources you could look into.

****

Chapter 4: What it Takes to Get Where You Want to Go

About this chapter

This chapter is all about what you need to do to make your goals a reality. We start by looking in more detail at how to work out your small steps. Then we look at preparing to succeed: what everyone can do to lay the foundations mentally and practically. Next you'll find out how you can identify the blocks that are stopping you from achieving your goals and how to do your research. Finally we do a goal check: do you need to achieve something else first or even something else *instead?*

This chapter assumes that you are able to use the internet. If you're not computer literate, then a short course on using the internet at your local library will widen your available research sources hugely. Take a small step today and sign up for one.

How to work out which small steps you need to take

Small steps to drinking a glass of water revisited

Relate it, reason it, revise it. Look back at the exercise called 'small steps practice' in chapter one. At the time, you wrote down the steps needed to drink a glass of water. Use them to practice the three Rs of the small steps method:

1. *Relate* the small steps you need to someone else or to yourself in a notebook. In this case, a flowchart, picture sequence or written steps on how to drink a glass of water.

2. *Reason* with yourself: do I need to go any further back or get more simple, more basic or more specific?

3. *Revise* your small steps: rewrite them or explain them again, adding any extra detail you need. Imagine you were

explaining the action to someone who had never done it before. Do the steps need revising?

You need to go further back than you think you do

Did you open the cupboard and get out a glass? Did you turn on the tap or open a bottle? Did you find some sand to make the material for your glass? Did you find someone who knows about glassmaking to help you? Did you employ a water-diviner? Or did you gather your neighbours together to dig a well? How did you purify the water? Just as you could keep taking a step back when it comes to drinking a glass of water, you can keep taking steps back with *any task you need to perform.*

You need to get smaller than you think you do

How specific did you go with the glass of water task? How long did you turn the tap on for? How clean was the glass? Just as you could keep getting more specific when it comes to drinking a glass of water, you can keep getting more specific with any task you need to perform, until you've literally written (or drawn!) yourself instructions. The harder – or more unfamiliar - the task, the closer you need to get to a list of simple written instructions.

Points to remember:

- If you think you're stuck you might need to take a few more steps back. Write down the task, take a step back, and another, and another until you get to the *most simple step.* Something you could do today.

- Or you might need to get even more specific. This is true with complicated or unfamiliar tasks, including tasks that are *emotionally* complicated or unfamiliar.

- Anything vague or unformed, anything you don't know how to do – leave a gap to fill in later or add the word 'research'.

Context is everything!
The people at the charity Water Aid describe themselves as follows: "Our mission is to transform lives by improving access to safe water, hygiene and sanitation in the world's poorest communities." Drinking a glass of water is simple – no need to break it down into steps. But for the people Water Aid helps every day, drinking a glass of water is far from straightforward. Your context – or your *big picture* - will inform how far back you need to go to get to your first small step. Your context will allow you to understand the specifics of your project.

For example, it would have been physically impossible for me to run a marathon just before having our baby! Recently a young woman called Amber Miller featured in the news because she had run the Chicago Marathon and had her baby – a healthy little girl called June - shortly afterwards. We're both new mums, but it's obvious that our contexts, and our levels of fitness, are very different.

Take some time to think about the environment, people, spaces, resources and things that surround you. Do they help or hinder you in achieving your goals and in your day-to-day life?

Prepare to succeed
Set yourself up for success.
Memory researchers say that we can usually hold about seven things in our short term memory at one time. How about trying to remember six? The six 'C's of setting up:

- Carry a notebook: We've already said you can use this to jot down ideas and to do the exercises in this book. Your notebook can be a computer or hand-held device – your choice. The important thing here is *carrying it with you* so that you can refer to it at odd moments, but more than that, so that it becomes your friend. Remember your pen, too.

- Cabinet or crate? Sort out your filing. Living with your papers in a mess is a big road block. Take a weekend to put everything you need in alphabetical order, to store it somewhere easy to access and to recycle (securely) what you don't need. Have a look at chapter fifteen for more on filing.

- Create (or identify) a space where you can work. Ideally this will be somewhere permanent that's just for you but even a tray next to your bed with a pen and notebook on it is a start. Ask people to treat it with respect.

- Clear the clutter. Another big road block is clutter. Take another weekend to identify what you really need. Is there anything you can sell online? Or anything you can list on recycling or swapping websites like freecycle? Or anything you can donate to charity? (Have a look at the resources section.)

The story of your success.
In this exercise, you look at how you have succeeded before and turn it into a story that you can use as a model for future achievements.

1. Think about a project or an area of your life where you succeeded, where you saw it through from beginning to end, where you were proud of yourself. Travel or study make good examples.

2. Can't think of anything? Ask someone close to you for an example.

3. Alternatively, you can create an achievement story for yourself right now. Take a goal from one area of your life and over the next few weeks do something – just *one thing* - towards achieving it. Use whatever you achieve to create your story of success.

4. Let the story you create be right for you. If you want to be a writer, signing up for an evening class is reason to congratulate yourself. We don't celebrate our achievements enough – especially not our small steps – and we should. A similar principle applies to people who are very driven. If you *have* run a marathon, written a novel, climbed Kilimanjaro, celebrate it! Very driven people tend not to give themselves time to take stock after each achievement. You can do that now by writing the story of your success.

5. Describe the story verbally to someone close to you or write it in your notebook: Where did you do it? How long did it take? What research did you have to do? What state of mind were you in during the project or once you had finished? What support did you receive?

We learn by making mistakes

Human beings have evolved to learn by making mistakes. The process of learning requires us to try something out, if it doesn't work, we try again, perfecting our skills along the way. If you know any babies or young children you can watch them learning like this. My son tried over and over again to crawl before he learned how to do it. The same thing happened when he learnt to walk. The idea of someone criticising him each time he 'failed' to crawl doesn't make any sense! But as adults this learning process gets scuppered when – because of criticism from ourselves or people around us – we give up at the first hurdle. It's been said many times that successful people aren't lucky. They just have a different attitude to failure. Several books have been written recently about the idea of talent (is it a myth?) and attitudes to success and failure. I review some of them in chapter seven. We'll also come back to this idea in chapter eight.

Just keep taking small steps

Your attitude to failure is important, but the small steps method stops it becoming a stumbling block. Let's go back to the prospective radio journalist at the beginning of the book. Rhonda emails three hospital radio stations and eventually volunteers at one. She 'fails' to get two of the volunteer positions she tries for, but it doesn't matter. One opportunity is all she needs. Instead of giving up after the first rejection, set back, or negative response, just keep taking small steps. For now, let go of the outcome.

For any task that seems too big or too complex or confusing to begin even, work out the first small step, then - without thinking about the prospect of success or failure for a moment – just work out another small step and another. You're not committing yourself to achieving them by writing them down.

Putting your success story to work

This is where you put past successes to work for you, so that you can use them to help you achieve your goals. In addition to the following, make time to read about other people's journeys to success. Pick people you admire and seek out any books they've written. You'll almost certainly find that the person you find inspiring didn't have a smooth ride to success, in fact the bumps along the road were an important part of the journey.

1. Look back at the story of your success. What were the key things that made you keep going until you succeeded?
2. Now think about a goal you want to achieve and look back at your success story. What would you need to do to apply

this story to your new goal? Is there anything missing this time that you had last time?

3. When you need a boost, focus on success stories like this one. These stories are so powerful because they are concrete examples from your own life.

4. Have a look at the books on success and perseverance reviewed in chapter seven, such at Carol S. Dweck's *Mindset*, Matthew Syed's *Bounce* and Tim Harford's *Adapt*.

What's getting in your way?

Self-criticism

It's all too easy to allow our internal critic to stop us from making progress. It trips us up because when we listen to it we don't want to learn from our mistakes. The more you hear your internal critic, the more likely it is you're trying something new.

Confirmation bias

Look down at the floor and close your eyes. Now think: "blue." Open your eyes and look around. What do you notice? Repeat the exercise with different colours. Try this before reading on.

Most people will notice the colour they thought about prior to opening their eyes. This also works with our attitudes about the world. If I metaphorically "look around" with the idea that the world is full of selfish people that's what I'll see. If I "look around" with the idea that nothing I do will succeed, my brain will obligingly look for evidence for me. This is an application of what psychologists call *confirmation bias*.

Identifying blocks

Here are some exercises that should enable you to identify the blocks that stop you from taking small steps towards achieving your goals. If you lack self-confidence or you are having trouble believing in the important projects you identified in chapter three, these are particularly pertinent:

1. Spend just one journey to work (perhaps not if you're driving!) thinking "leaves are fascinating" or "everyone has a secret" or "people in this town are always smiling" – did you notice confirmation bias in action? See if you can pick up on any kind of *negative* confirmation bias in your day-to-day life.

2. You've probably heard of the saying "smile and the world smiles with you" but did you know that it is literally true? Try smiling at everyone you meet. Yes, some people won't react, but most of them will. A demonstration of the idea that it only takes a small change in attitude to start seeing the world differently!

3. Spend a week noticing your internal critic. Just observe – don't respond one way or the other. Make notes in your notebook. Be ready to laugh at it, rather than arguing with it. Remember that even the most successful people have an internal critic – it's nothing to do with how much you've achieved.

4. In your notebook make a list of the things that are stopping you from making progress. This could be physical, financial, practical or emotional blocks, or knowledge gaps. Be as specific as you can.

5. Is your problem *really* your problem? Think particularly of your environment and those around you. For example, one student I taught was convinced she had writer's block. After questioning her, I discovered that her neighbours were renovating their house and she was trying to write to the sound of them knocking down walls. She had another problem too: she didn't have any confidence in her abilities. As soon as she created a quiet space to work somewhere else,

her writer's block disappeared and her confidence grew – but she had to do it that way round. This is small steps principle number 8 in action. She gained confidence from turning up and from writing one page at a time.

More on confirmation bias
Wishing for buses at the North Pole

You might have heard of the 'law of attraction'. The alluring idea - though very difficult to square for anyone with a social conscience – that we get what we attract. Simply state what you want, so proponents of this law tell us, and the universe will provide. It's possible that the idea of a law of attraction is simply confirmation bias in action.

Remember Rhonda, the prospective radio journalist from chapter two? I pointed out then that just as you're more likely to get on a bus if you stand at a bus stop, you're more likely to meet a sports broadcaster if you're at a radio station? If you stand at a bus stop and wish like mad for a bus to come, eventually your wish will come true. You're also *more likely* to wish for a bus at a bus stop. In fact, if you think about it, bus stops are the concrete result of a large group of people 'wishing' really hard for buses. You could call that 'magic' or you could call it civilisation organising itself.

If you wish for a bus at the North Pole, you might meet a TV crew making a documentary about polar bears or a scientist researching global warming, but it would be a very unlikely that you'd see a red double-decker London bus, no matter how hard you wished for it. So put yourself at a bus stop if you want a bus or near the North Pole if you want to research polar bears, but make sure you've got bus fair or a very warm coat first. Just like Rhonda put herself at a hospital radio station because she wanted a career in broadcast journalism, decide where you need to put yourself to make your goals a reality and find the most simple, cheapest and easiest way to get there.

Use confirmation bias to your advantage
It's possible to use confirmation bias to your advantage. Focus on what you want, and as long as your basic needs are met (read more on Maslow's *Hierarchy of Needs* in chapter one and chapter thirteen) and you'll start to notice it, just like you see pink cars everywhere if you walk near a road thinking 'pink cars'. Spend time thinking about work experience, getting published or eating healthily and you'll start to notice opportunities to do just that: but only if you get up off the sofa.

Doing your research
Identifying your research tasks
When you created your flowcharts in chapter three, you added the word 'research' to any vague or unformed ideas. In the example, a vague idea about teaching abroad became 'research teaching abroad.' You didn't commit yourself, you simply made the first step concrete. Your reaction to that first small step gave you a clue about whether you really did want to take it further.

Research can take many different forms. Spending time in libraries, bookshops and museums, or at employment fairs and networking events, chatting with colleagues and using social media are all examples of research.

Look back through your notebook. Anytime you've added 'research' to an idea, decide whether it's still important, and, if it is, highlight it and add it to a list of research tasks.

Research exercises to get you started
This is the point where you start working on those research tasks.

You can download a note on using a search engine from the Small Steps website.

1. Take one unformed idea. Something that seems attractive but out of reach. Something you know little about. Where can you get information and advice on this particular thing? What other sources of information and advice exist? If you don't know, try some blanket networking. Ask everyone you think might be able to help – people who can be trusted with the idea of course – where you can get more information. Ask in libraries. Use the internet. This will generate some leads. Schedule some time to follow up these leads.

2. Extend your available sources of advice and information. Do you *always* use libraries first, or a search engine, or do you chat to people first? Try the alternatives. At first, take every opportunity to extend your available sources. You can do this using bibliographies in books on the topic, well-run websites, experts in a field. Go outside your comfort zone. By 'experts' I mean people with years of experience – anyone can set themselves up as an 'expert' on the internet so check the credentials. Publication or acknowledgement from a professional body are good signs that experts know their stuff.

3. Exploit your weak contacts. The theory goes that you probably use the same resources as the people you know well. You go to similar places, like similar things and know about the same events. People you don't know very well – friends of friends - will tap into a similar network involving the people *they* know well. The best way to find out about the resources available to these so-called weak contacts is to ask directly.

4. Nowadays you can use social media to exploit weak contacts and ask if anyone has any relevant expertise. If you have a

lot of 'friends' on a social media network, many will be weak contacts anyway. You might still have to ask people specifically, though, as a general plea will only generate a handful of (often unhelpful) comments.

5. Deeper research. Go back to that unformed, vague idea. You still don't have to commit long term. This time you're going to dip your toe in the water to see how you like it. Go on an introductory course, spend a day in the library reading about it, try some aspect of it that you haven't tried before, visit someone who knows a lot about it. If we *only* do internet research, we often get stuck and don't take any action. This kind of research forces you to *do something* related to your goal.

6. Be objective. At this point, try to put aside your emotional response to this goal. Review your research so far. What are the main steps to achieving this goal? Remove emotional content or context. No implications this time. Just write down the steps. If it helps, imagine someone else is going to do it, and you're telling them how.

7. Do you need to make your goal bigger? Perhaps your research has shown up that you're limiting yourself too much. Is lack of confidence holding you back? Do you need to expand your ideas?

8. Did your research put you off? Change your mind! It's ok to go back to the drawing board. That's what research is for: to enable you to find out what you're in for if you follow this path.

What do you need to achieve *first*? What do you need to achieve *instead*?

What do you need to achieve first?
Take some time to consider these questions:

- What other goals lead to your goal?
- How much money will you need?
- What qualifications do you need?
- Is 'achieve this first' standing in your way? Is it really a problem?
- Could you volunteer?

What other goals lead to your goal?
This is often about getting more specific. If you want to start your own business, 'complete a course in business skills' is a goal that might lead to your goal. Take an honest look at your goals and at where you are now. If you want to publish an article, it's not a good idea to go to the huge national and international magazines first. Start local with your student magazine or a special interest publication.

How much money will you need?
Look at all related costs and how you will pay for them. Include them in a formal document, not on the back of an envelope. Look at upfront financial outlay, ongoing costs, and costs in terms of the time you'll need to invest. Next, plan to do anything that is free first before you fully commit yourself. This, of course, still has a time cost, but probably a limited one. This goes for taster courses, time spent in the library, and 'free' market research carried out amongst friends, colleagues and weak contacts.

What qualifications do you need?
Think broadly. If you want to start a cake making business, you might already be proficient at baking cupcakes, but you'll need a certificate in food hygiene. And do you know enough about marketing to take your idea forward?

Is 'achieve this first' standing in your way?

Sometimes – as a form of procrastination - we tell ourselves we need to achieve something first before we can complete our goal and it's actually an excuse. You might need to jump in and have a go instead.

Could you volunteer?

Nothing beats interaction with people doing what you want to do, even if it's only tangentially related. It gets you out of your usual routine and helps you to think differently, but I mention it here primarily because it's an excellent networking opportunity. Look back at the example about the prospective radio journalist in chapter 2. You can see how many networking opportunities come up as a result of an initially small investment of time. The illustration in chapter 2 is not the only way into this particular career, of course. Neither is it a straight uncomplicated path into broadcast journalism, but remember: one small step does not necessarily have to lead to the next as long as they link back to the original goal. The fictional trainee journalist seeks out a new source of information or advice everywhere she goes.

What do you need to achieve instead?

This is the flipside of the previous advice on what you need to achieve first. It's a chance to review your goals once more to make sure they are exactly as you want them. Take some time to consider these questions:

- Are there any goals left on the list that you think you 'should' do?
- Do any of your goals seem tedious? Where's the fun gone?
- Could you spend more time with the people you love? Could you spend more time interacting with people?
- What would you rather do?

Take out the 'should'

Here's another chance to make sure that these are *your* goals and not someone else's! At the start of term, we tell our writing students to make a list of their passions and beliefs and to write about them. Six weeks later we check drafts of their stories. Many of them will have abandoned their passions for what they think we want them to write, even though they spent an entire class at the start of term learning about why writers need to write what they love. The best stories are the ones where the writer has dared to ignore the *should*. The same goes for goal setting.

Make your goal more fun

Does the goal seem tedious? It might be a sign that you don't really want to do it. Alternatively, you might have sucked the fun out of it as you turned it into a goal! Get back to what you really love about this area of your life. What's fun about this activity? Make a point of doing something fun – something that's related to this goal - before the end of the week. Think creatively. You might think there's nothing fun about the goal to 'become better at maths' until you play numbers games with your kids. Perhaps you don't want to turn your hobby into a business after all because you want to keep it strictly for pleasure.

Build relationships with other people

One of the best ways to get a sense of ourselves and what we want in life is to interact with others. Make a point of spending time doing something simple with people you love and consider signing up for a leisure activity or sport that involves regular contact with other people. Once you've done that, check in with your goals and one more time (we're gearing up for the next chapter) ask yourself: what would you rather do?

Key points

In this chapter we've covered:

1. How to work out which small steps you need to take using the three Rs: relate it, reason it, revise it.
2. Considering your context.
3. Setting yourself up for success with the six Cs : Carry a notebook; cabinet or crate; create a space; clear the clutter.
4. Writing the story of your success.
5. Learning by mistakes.
6. Identifying blocks.
7. The 'law of attraction' and confirmation bias.
8. Deciding where you need to put yourself to make your goals a reality.
9. Doing your research.
10. What do you need to achieve *first*? What do you need to achieve *instead*?

****

Chapter 5: Reality Check

About this chapter

This chapter is dedicated to giving your goals a reality check. Yes, we've been trying to do that as we go along – and we had a goal check at the end of the last chapter - but here we look at reality checking in more detail. It's something that many goal setting books don't include and it's not intended to put a dampener on your dreams. Rather, we can loosely sum up the advice in this chapter with what's become known as the alcoholic's prayer:

> "God grant us the serenity to accept the things we cannot change, courage to change the things we can, and wisdom to know the difference." - Reinhold Niebuhr

The Alcoholic's Prayer

Two caveats to the usual goal setting advice

A goal assumes you want to change something in your life. The *Alcoholic's Prayer* suggests that there are some things we can change and some things we can't – some things we can set goals for and some we're better off forgetting. We need wisdom to tell the difference, or a blunt and honest look at ourselves. As I said, many books on goal setting leave out this step, urging readers to do anything in their power to achieve their goals. But there are two important caveats which they seem to forget, and they're important if you're going to give your goals a reality check:

1. Would you really do *anything* to achieve this goal? Some things may be more important than this goal. It depends what it is. You can be pretty certain that a goal like 'stop smoking by the end of the year' has almost no downsides.

But would you really risk losing your friends and family or your health in pursuit of a goal?

2. In an age that celebrates so-called eternal youth and the power of the individual whilst telling us we can achieve anything we want to, there are actually some things you can't do.

Not qualifying for the Olympics: different goals for different people
This is the secret behind the Alcoholic's Prayer: pin point what you *genuinely* need or want to change. I'm never going to qualify for the Olympics. I'm not doing myself a disservice by admitting it and it doesn't matter how hard I apply myself or how many times I say positive affirmations. It's not all or nothing: Given that almost *everyone* will improve their lives by exercising a bit more, I'll still improve my life if I exercise more regularly.

During the summer I decided to start exercising again. Looking at my son, I knew I wanted to be fit and healthy enough both to look after him and to watching him grow up. This is a big deal for me because it requires a change of attitude. For me, 'Exercise three times a week' is a much better goal than 'Win a medal at the Olympics.' Remember Amber Miller who gave birth after running a marathon? In a BBC interview she described herself as "crazy about running". Her goals are going to be very different from mine. By the way, if you *are* a prospective Olympian: good luck!

The wisdom to tell the difference?
So you're giving your goals a reality check: but how do you tell the difference between what you can change and what you can't or what you need to change and what you don't? First, get up off the sofa and *do something*. For example, I saw a nurse before I started exercising again. Amber Miller spoke to a doctor before entering the

Chicago Marathon. Make it something small, but something concrete. Have you:

- Spoken to an expert, or if it's relevant, seen a doctor?
- Been on a short course?
- Spoken to someone who's already achieved it?
- Done your research? Do you know enough about it to know whether this goal is for you?
- Accepted your limitations?
- Re-read the story of your success?

Risk assessment

Low risk? Jump in!

The next stage in giving your goals a reality check is a risk assessment. You might be used to doing risk assessments at work but this is more personal. Firstly, bear in mind that it's best to jump in and try something *if* the risks and the costs are limited. Ideally, seek out the opportunity to jump in and try something for a short amount of time with low risk involvement. For example, if you want to write comedy or screenplays, try a week at the Arvon Foundation. Your risk is limited to the cost of the course, potentially a week's annual leave entitlement, and a week of your own time. Plus if it's not for you, you might have to face up to any family and friends you've told. Conversely, *don't* commit a large amount of time and money to a project without considering the implications.

Your risk assessment

At this stage of the reality check, ask yourself the following questions and write down the answers in your notebook:

- What are the financial implications? What initial steps can I take for free? How much will it cost if I continue? Be careful here: buying equipment or paying course fees isn't the same as achieving your goal.

- What are the risks to the other areas of your life?
- What else is important? What is *more* important?
- Any health implications?
- Have you discussed it with your family or friends?
- Can you make the time and space?
- Can you make the commitment?

You might not need to commit (yet)

My favourite quotation about commitment comes from a book about exploring:

> Until one is committed, there is hesitancy, the chance to draw back, always ineffectiveness. Concerning all acts of initiative (and creation), there is one elementary truth the ignorance of which kills countless ideas and splendid plans: that the moment one definitely commits oneself, the providence moves too. A whole stream of events issues from the decision, raising in one's favour all manner of unforeseen incidents, meetings and material assistance, which no man could have dreamt would have come his way. - W. H. Murray.

Once you commit, the magic starts to happen: the kind of magic that's a result of your determination to succeed. In the section on confirmation bias in the previous chapter, I suggested that if you close your eyes and think of a colour, when you open your eyes, you'll see that colour. Your brain looks for what you tell it to look for, so if you commit yourself, your brain will look for opportunities to fulfil that commitment. It feels like magic, and in a way it is: everyday magic. *But* you don't have to commit until you're ready. It's possible to plan first, to do your research and look at your options before committing, because that kind of preparation frees you up to think about possibilities without the frightening prospect of them becoming reality (yet). Make sure you watch out for the moment when it is time to commit.

The impossible dream paradox
Dream the impossible or get more specific?
This is a conundrum. We're told we need to let ourselves dream, to imagine the impossible, but *honestly speaking* is that really an option? Doesn't that kind of advice lead to disillusionment and cynicism?

Does it matter when a goal seems impossible, improbable or deluded? Here's the problem - and paradoxically those who recommend 'blue sky thinking' suffer from it too – impossible dreams are often too general, too broad, too wishy-washy. Books on goal setting are usually too general because they have to cater for all kinds of goals. Telling someone to 'dream the impossible' is too general: how on earth do you implement that kind of advice?

What we need, as a solution to the impossible dream paradox, is a big dose of honesty and a big dose of specificity. Get more specific. Often when stated specifically, a goal is no longer impossible, improbable or deluded – but it still would cost us something to achieve it. Once it's made specific we can work out that cost.

Who says?
Who told you the dream was impossible? If it was someone very significant - a parent, a teacher, a partner – then it is hard to be objective. How much did they know about it? How has their own life experience limited their outlook? Again, getting as specific as possible about the steps you would need to take and the time and money you would need to invest will help remove the mysticism around this apparently impossible dream. They might be right.

59

They might not be. If you're really not sure, test it out by breaking this goal down into its component parts until you get to something you could achieve today.

What are the consequences?

If you had achieved this goal what would the rest of your life look like? In chapter one we used the life parts health, career, study, family, finances, travel, leisure, social. In the first exercise in chapter three you made up your own list of life parts. Use either as a checklist to work out the consequences. Make sure that you have included the emotional consequences, which can be overlooked.

In planning to achieve a goal you do take a risk: you risk failure. You risk having to face up to the idea that you tried but it didn't work. Usually – it depends on the goal – the journey makes that risk worthwhile, but it's worth looking this one square in the face before you start.

Dream big

Specific doubts and specific goals

The latest life improvement guru tells us that we're 'thinking too small' or that we should 'think big' but isn't that also too general to be useful? Well, yes, but sometimes lack of confidence *does* make us put psychological barriers up. What's the solution? *Get specific* again and turn a specific doubt into an achievable goal. It's possible to learn to do all of the following things and / or to get expert help. What each one needs is an investment of *time*:

> "I could never start a cake-making business, I don't know anything about marketing".

> "I could never teach in Germany, I'm terrible with languages".

"I'll never have a baby because the doctor says I have to lose weight first".

The biggest version of your goal
This is a practical exercise designed to help you talk yourself out of barriers such as these.

1. As a way of making 'thinking big' an achievable task, try inventing the BIGGEST version of your goal. Write it down. Have fun with it. We've dealt with the serious side, now you can play:

   "My cake-making business dominates the UK market in cup cakes."

   "I learn five languages and travel around the world giving master classes in my subject."

   "I joined a weigh-loss programme and have started a family. Now I give advice on weight-loss, fertility and family planning."

2. Can you get even bigger? (Notice that these get more specific as they get bigger, and not less specific.)

   "I write a series of books on cake making and become a celebrity baker, making regular appearances on television. I become known internationally as an expert in both home start up businesses and cake decoration. I take on trainees each year who are specially chosen from the long-term unemployed."

"I am a multilingual expert in my subject, training thousands of other people to teach it. I set up academies the world over using my specially developed learning and teaching style. Many of my teachers go into schools up and down the country to start language clubs for young people."

"I have adopted four children and had two myself. I run a business helping women to get fit for pregnancy. I have marketed the franchise internationally and so far I have helped thousands of women to have a baby or to live a fulfilling life without children. I donate a portion of my profits to women running start-up ventures in the developing world."

What you'll notice when you make your dreams bigger like this is that when you get specific they no longer feel vague and unformed. Maybe you don't want to achieve the biggest version of your dream but if you've worked through the material in this book so far you should now know how to work out the small steps you'd need to follow in order to get there. You might realise that this goal isn't after all what you want, or what you're able to achieve. That's ok too.

3. What's the *first* small step required to realise your so-called impossible dream? Keep getting smaller until you find something you could do today.
    "My first small step was enrolling on a free course for new business women run by the local council. Actually it all started when I picked up a leaflet in the library."
    "My first small step? I have a good friend who speaks German, who went back to college. We worked out a skills exchange. He needed help with his essays and in return he helped me to learn his mother-tongue. It all started when I

invited myself to dinner and his very large family were chatting away in German."

"I'd say my first small step was making that first phone call to a weight loss counsellor. It all started when I got brave enough to pick up the phone."

Testing your goals
Your reality check

Go through the list of goals you made in chapter three. Now you've read the chapter on reality checking, do you need to make any changes? Are any irrelevant? Unachievable? Some (seemingly) impossible goals are ok – but try making them as specific as you possibly can. Have some concrete smaller goals too. If you have few big dreams, introduce some, or make one or two of your goals bigger. If you have few concrete smaller goals, set some now or make some smaller. Come back to this reality check as regularly as you need to, or whenever your goals get too general and vague.

Key points
In this chapter, we have covered:

1. The Alcoholic's Prayer.
2. Two caveats to the usual goal setting advice.
3. Not qualifying for the Olympics: different goals for different people.
4. Your risk assessment.
5. The impossible dream paradox and getting more specific.
6. Who told you the dream was impossible?
7. What are the consequences of achieving your impossible dream?
8. Dreaming big.
9. The BIGGEST version of your goal.
10. Testing your goals: your reality check.

Chapter 6: The Pursuit of Happiness

About this chapter

Happiness is a hot topic. Governments are beginning to use happiness measures in the same way that economics are used as an indication of standards of living. What almost everyone who has looked into happiness agrees is that it's an elusive term to describe. This chapter asks the question: is happiness the ultimate goal? We begin by looking at different ways of measuring happiness, followed by different definitions of what happiness actually is and what you can do about it. Then we move on to looking at how other people are involved in our happiness. How can groups of people be happy? The amount of support you get *and* the amount of autonomy you have affect your happiness. How do you treasure your own autonomy *and* build direct and indirect support for your goals? This chapter gives you practical exercises to try and suggestions for small steps you can take to improve your own happiness and to build your support network.

What people are saying about happiness

The comparison paradox

We know that happiness is relative: happiness often depends on comparisons of our lives with that of those around us. Further, deep happiness may result from *loosening* the ties that bind our happiness to these comparisons, and *strengthening* the ties that connect us, genuinely, with other people.

Dr Happiness

According to *Time Magazine*, Professor Ed Diener is also known as Dr Happiness, such is his influence on happiness research. He was asked in a BBC interview in 2006 about the key ingredients for long term happiness. His big three are given below. Number three is particularly important for us!

1. social relationships,
2. having some meaning in your life,
3. working towards goals that you enjoy, and that reflect your values

There's more on Ed Diener in the resources section.

The importance of autonomy

According to research by social scientists at the University of Michigan, autonomy – feeling that we have some control over our lives – is the most important factor when it comes to our happiness levels.

Happiness and pleasure

Psychologists and neuroscientists have also noted that there is a difference between a state of happiness and an experience which gives us pleasure. It follows that we might go through something unpleasant in order to be happy. Some argue that, paradoxically, we need to experience both difficult and uplifting events in life in order to achieve true happiness.

Different happiness measures

Gross National Happiness or GNH.

This is the concept, originating in Bhutan, that the happiness of a nation can be measured just as the Gross Domestic Product (GDP) can be measured. In fact, proponents claim it gives a better indication of happiness and wellbeing than using a purely economic model. One proposal for testing GNH takes in:

- Economic wellness
- Environmental wellness
- Physical wellness
- Mental wellness

- Workplace wellness
- Social wellness
- Political wellness

Your Better Life Index

The Organisation for Economic Co-operation and Development (or OECD) has created a 'Better Life' index, which compares eleven areas that are key to people's wellbeing across different countries . You can see this in action on the interactive 'Your Better Life Index' website. The suggestion here is that i) society-wide factors affect our happiness levels ii) improving these eleven areas would increase people's happiness. The eleven topics compared by the OECD are:

- Community
- Education
- Environment
- Governance
- Health
- Housing
- Income
- Jobs
- Life Satisfaction
- Safety
- Work / Life Balance

The Happiness Index

An ongoing survey, commissioned by the UK government, is attempting to discover how happy we are in Britain. The Office for National Statistics (ONS) began by asking 200,000 people the following questions, which participants scored out of ten:

- How satisfied are you with your life nowadays? •
- How happy did you feel yesterday?
- How anxious did you feel yesterday? •

- To what extent do you feel the things you do in your life are worthwhile?

Finding out more

There are a number of books and websites on happiness that go into more detail than I have space for here. Some of these are recommended in the resources. A read through the quotations on the Positive Psychology Center website will give you plenty of food for thought for example.

Different kinds of happiness

Can money buy happiness?

Not having much money (or being worried about money) can make you very unhappy but financial security and happiness are not the same thing. Not everyone is motivated by money. Many people are motivated by friends, family or spirituality, for example. Conversely, striving for financial security provides some people with motivation to work, which gives meaning to their lives. Winning the lottery would spell disaster for them. For these people, money is a motivation, just not a direct one. Some commentators argue that happiness results from being paid about the same amount as people you know, having a similar number of possessions, living in a comparative sized house. In other words, happiness is equated with financial stability and comparability.

A happy old age

When some people talk about happiness, they are literally talking about a specific future in which they are able to 'retire happy'. Happiness to them means financial security, good health and good relationships into old age. From this point of view it is worth making sacrifices now to achieve happiness. It's worth thinking about what this would mean to you.

Acquiring something we don't have

It's possible to invest one particular thing we perceive as lacking from our lives with happiness. If only I had X – a stable relationship, a house, a round the world ticket, a job, a baby – I would be happy. This isn't just frippery - it might be true - although it would be tempting to start craving the next thing I don't have after acquiring the original! The trouble with this way of thinking is that we miss the possibility for happiness now, and we miss out on enjoying and learning from the journey.

Mindfulness

The concept the Buddhists call Mindfulness means being aware in each moment. You don't have to be Buddhist to benefit from Mindfulness. According to this theory, it's dangerous to assume that we will reach a happy point somewhere in some vague future once all our goals are achieved.

It's the word 'pursuit' in 'the pursuit of happiness' that is misleading. We don't have to pursue anything. Each moment is enough just as it is. Tara Brach's *Radical Acceptance* – reviewed in chapter seven - explains this concept further.

Is happiness the hidden goal behind all other goals?

Is 'I want to be happy' the ultimate hidden goal behind all of our goals? On the one hand, if all of your goals *don't* ultimately lead to happiness - which, according to happiness experts, isn't the same as instant pleasure or freedom from challenges - is there any sense in pursuing them? On the other hand, it is very difficult to define happiness. Setting goals is one way to make sure that you are doing what you want to be doing in life – you don't yet know if they will somehow 'make you happy' in the future.

What can you do about it?

If you've followed the suggestions so far in this book and you've been honest about setting goals, you've already taken steps towards creating a happy life, now and in the future. Here are some other suggestions:

- Read some of the happiness literature listed in the resources section.
- Find out about mindfulness.
- Decide how much you are equating happiness with i) financial security; ii) some point in the future – either vague or specific; iii) pleasure; iv) something you don't have.
- Define happiness i) for yourself; ii) with those closest to you.

Making other people happy

Feel like a doormat?

'I've spent my life making other people happy'. This idea is often used as a negative, as if we can't become happy at the same time. What's wrong with making other people happy? In fact, making other people happy is genuinely happiness-creating, as long as the relationship is reciprocal – you get a lot out of it too. If you've spent your life making other people happy, congratulate yourself – it's a wonderful thing to do. If what you really mean is 'I've spent my life being a doormat' or 'I'm taken for granted', here are some suggestions:

- Have another look at the section on 'the story of your success' in chapter four. The problem might be that you need to reframe how you think about the world.
- If you really do feel that you've been walked on all your life, take a small step: do one thing today that is just for you and no one else, even if it's having a

bath or going for a walk or sitting down to read a magazine. Do something just for you every day from now on and keep a note of it in your notebook.

- We often underestimate the importance of healthy eating and exercise on our mental health. This is part of looking after yourself. Take a small step today: make a healthy meal for yourself or go swimming at your local pool.

- Make a list of things you appreciate as often as possible. Do it before you go to bed or on your journey to work. People I do this exercise with are usually surprised at how long their list grows, once they give themselves permission to fill the page.

- You can also try being direct, and asking people you trust for appreciation. Be honest. "I'm feeling low today, tell me something you appreciate about me."

- There are assertiveness courses available at most community colleges. Take another small step and sign up for one.

Happy teams

Selfish individuals perform better than altruistic individuals, but altruistic groups perform better than selfish groups. This is taken from evolutionary biology, but I'm going to borrow it and change the meaning (with unreserved apologies to all evolutionary biologists), as follows: if you work in a group where everyone behaves altruistically towards one another, that group will out-perform groups of people who are behaving selfishly towards one another.

This is most relevant, in our context, to families and to teams who need to work together.

Practical suggestions for building altruistic groups

The difficulty here is to build an environment where people are *able* to act altruistically towards one another and where they trust each other enough to do so. People's *total* need has to be considered and their *total* skillset taken into consideration: not just those needs and skills that they regularly bring to the group. This will take training and can't be solved using a quick fix – one day spent doing trust building exercises is not only embarrassing but it won't achieve very much. I suggest starting by:

- Reading more about Maslow's *Hierarchy of Needs*. See chapters one and thirteen and the bonus bit on the website.
- Being honest and direct about the aims of the group.
- Having regular meetings. Allow everyone to be heard.
- Making sure everyone has somewhere to put their things (somewhere they belong).
- Allowing everyone in the group to have input into the way rewards and sanctions are administered. Reward reciprocal skill-sharing behaviour or anything the group defines as 'non-selfish'.
- With an experienced trainer, try drawing a figure of each person in the group and surrounding the figure with images or words describing his or her needs and skills.

Support from others, supporting others
Direct and indirect support

There are two kinds of support when it comes to goal setting: direct support, for example, attending a NHS Stop Smoking group, and indirect support, for example, the support we get from friends and family. Sometimes just having someone to hang out with is enough. We don't have to tell everybody and anybody about our goals.

Dependence and autonomy?

So we know that researchers have discovered that both social relationships *and* the amount of autonomy you have affect your happiness. In addition, research has shown that it is easier to achieve specific goals if we get some support. In other words, it's important that we can make choices and have control over our lives; it's also important that we depend on others. You can treasure your own autonomy *and* build direct and indirect support for your goals. How? By being proactive, and you can be proactive by taking small steps.

Support for my goal: a practical exercise

Try this exercise. Take one of your goals. Create a spider diagram showing the support you will need to achieve your goal. Write the goal in the middle of the sheet of paper. Put a circle around it. Who are you relying on to allow you to achieve this goal? Add more circles with names, and connect them to your goal. For example, if you need a loan to start a business, that's direct support: add the bank's small business advisor to your diagram. Add people who offer indirect support. For example, if your parents look after your children once a week, and indirectly support your goal, they go onto the diagram.

Do you know about the dreams, ambitions, hopes and fears of any of the people on your diagram? Probably only if they are close friends or family members or if you know the career aims of any colleagues on your list. Do you notice any opportunities to create a reciprocal relationship, where you can offer support in return? Do you notice any clashes between their goals and yours? For example, if you rely on your parents for childcare once a week, that would interfere with their ambition to sail around the world.

Interdependence v. Independence

In a sense, everyone is *dependent:* it is almost impossible to achieve our goals independently. We need support from other people, directly and indirectly. We need to work with and trust other people. That's a good thing. It makes the journey more rewarding. We can, however, be *independent* in the sense that we're individually responsible for our actions and reactions and for planning our lives. That's also a good thing.

For example, when trying to achieve my goal to exercise three times a week, it was a huge help when I found a really good teacher. By really good, I don't mean good at sport, though I imagine she is that too. I mean a really good *teacher.* I'm not friends with her; I hardly ever speak to her, but she's inspiring and motivating and crucially for me *doesn't get in the least bit annoyed with me.* You might have to try a few exercise classes before you find a good teacher – don't give up!

Supporting others

For a holistic approach, caring for the people who are close to us, and knowing about their dreams as well as their more everyday goals, must be part of any goal you take on. No goal will lead to happiness without this aspect. It's a part of the process that many goal setting techniques ignore. It is crucial not only to have the support of people around you, but to support them in return.

Co-dependence

Co-dependence – a word much used by therapists – is when we don't take responsibility for ourselves. If you've got this far through the book and you've been working through the exercises, you've gone a long way towards taking responsibility for your future, but if you think your relationships with others are getting in the way of your happiness, there are plenty of small steps suggested in this chapter to help you. You might also want to seek help from a counsellor.

The importance of friendship

Don't underestimate the importance of having friends around you. Loneliness makes you unhappy. It can become a vicious circle. The more lonely we feel, the more withdrawn we can become. Loneliness can distort your sense of what's important in life, so that it's hard to work out what your goals are, and it can also stop you from achieving them. The flipside can also be true. Stopping at nothing to achieve our goals might lead to loneliness. If any of this strikes a chord with you, take some of the small steps listed below.

How to find direct support:

- Take a small step today: if it's relevant, find out about a support group you can join to help you achieve your goal.
- For a health or career-related goal there are likely to be formal groups advertising on the internet, at work, in the local library or in your GP's Surgery.
- Think creatively. For example, if your goal is to find a life partner, joining a book group or a wine tasting club might allow you to meet people with similar interests.
- Some direct support will be one-on-one: with a nutritionist, a careers advisor or a fitness instructor, for example.
- One-to-one support doesn't have to be expensive. Some people will qualify for free support through the NHS.

- Return to the list of skills you wrote in the very first chapter during the activity suggested under '*Do you need a goal?*' Could you swap skills with someone? There are skills exchange websites listed in the resources section.
- With direct support, the activity of the group will be related to your goal somehow.

How to build a wider support network:

- Try this. You need a blank sheet of paper. Draw a diagram with yourself in the middle. At the top write "my support network". Add anyone you consider part of your wider support network, whether you are related or not. Take your time. Add everyone you think is relevant.
- Grateful list time! Spend some time writing a grateful list specifically about the people in your life. What do you appreciate most about the people around you?
- Be proactive. Organise social events for your existing friends.
- Sometimes we need deliberately to build new friendships. Again return to the list of skills you wrote. Could you teach or develop any of these as a way of making contact with people?
- Either take an interest you already have and research ways of meeting people through it or find a new interest and join a group that welcomes beginners.
- Try to pick an established group that organises social events (check the website) as well as their regular sessions or rehearsals or training. For example, a sports team, a choir, a meditation group, a

performing arts group. You might like to take a friend with you to the first session.

- When you're building a wider support network, the activity probably won't be related to your goal. Instead it will give you a break from your goal.

Goal check: what does happiness look like?

- Your happiness picture. With your eyes closed, visualise what happiness looks like, specifically, for you.
- What will it take for you to be happy today, in one week, one month, one year, five years and in ten years? Again, visualise what happiness looks like.
- Your partner's happiness picture. Ask your partner or the person closest to you to repeat this exercise so you can compare results.
- Goal check. Now look back at the goals you've written down. Do your goals fit your happiness picture?

Key Points

In this chapter, we've covered:

1. What people are saying about happiness
2. Different happiness measures
3. Different kinds of happiness
4. Making other people happy
5. Happy teams
6. Practical suggestions for building altruistic groups
7. Support for my goal / supporting others
8. The importance of friendship
9. Direct and indirect support
10. Goal check: what does happiness look like?

Chapter 7: A Review of Goal Setting Methods, Including the Goal-Free Method

About this chapter

In this chapter I've taken some of the most popular goal setting resources around and have divided them into categories according to their themes and ideas. These categories are my invention. The categories are somewhat artificial as there is some overlap, but the intention is to show you what's out there. If you do want to take any of these ideas further, I've done some of the hard work for you, so you don't have to search too far for the materials that are right for you. The categories are:

- The productivity, work or sales method
- The habits of success method
- The life-roles or whole self method
- The mistakes and perseverance method
- The journey-focused method

You'll find details on all of the books and resources mentioned in the final section of this book. Because the methods reviewed here involve motivating people to succeed, many of them come in different forms: websites, motivational speakers, workshops, CDs, videos as well as books. Most of them require you to follow some kind of programme or do some exercises to participate. The choice can seem overwhelming. Remember these reviews contain my subjective opinion. There's no substitute for trying any appealing ideas out for yourself but you certainly don't need to read or participate in all of them in order to succeed. Most people find it's better to pick one or two methods that work – which might take a bit of trial and error – and to *practise*. Beware of anything offering results in 24 hours!

The productivity, work or sales method
What is it?

These goal setting methods tend to be focused on motivation in the workplace. In this category, you'll find books and programmes for managers who want to motivate their employees as well as books for individuals who want to find a job they love. The ideas are often related to jobs that involve selling. These are the goal setting methods that you might see satirised in film comedies, but that doesn't mean that none of the techniques will work for you.

At their worst they can be focused on a very narrow definition of 'success' and encourage adherents to stop at nothing to get what they want. This means they sometimes don't consider the whole person and the techniques suggested can therefore feel rather flimsy.

At their best, they help people to become more assertive in a work situation and to find work that motivates them. One could argue that everyone needs to be able to 'sell' something, at least in its broadest sense: a teacher convincing a parent to read to his children is selling the idea that reading is important, a neighbourhood campaign to raise money for a community centre has to sell the idea to supporters. One could also argue that because almost everyone works (though not necessarily in paid work, something these types of books sometimes forget) any well-written guide to getting the most out of your working life is potentially useful as long as it takes in the bigger picture.

Brian Tracey

Brian Tracey is a management consultant, bestselling author and motivational speaker. His books aren't subtle. Goals! is emblazed in large letters across the cover of the book with that title, and has the tag-line *Get Everything You Want – Faster Than You Ever Dreamed* and I couldn't avoid feeling that I was being shouted at when I read it. The book does contain useful advice and practical exercises. For example, Tracey's "seven keys to goal setting" can be usefully applied to any goal, if they appeal to you. According to chapter six of Tracey's book, you need to make goals "specific", "measurable", time limited, "challenging", value-bound and "balanced". Plus, all of your goals should move you towards an overarching life goal. This is similar to SMART goal-setting: Specific, Measurable, Achievable, Results-Orientated and Time-limited. Of course, that's all very well, as long as it's possible to add 'desirable' or even 'enjoyable' to the mix!

Tracey has inspired thousands of people but if you find management-speak or constant positivity even faintly annoying, this may not be the book for you – try the 'journey-focused' method instead. I was left feeling that it might be better, after all, to 'get some of what you want' slowly or not to 'get everything you want' but to enjoy the journey.

Who else writes about it?
- Zig Ziglar. Ziglar is another motivational speaker from the US, who speaks particularly about selling and work-related performance strategies. He has produced books and CDs and you can hear him speak on YouTube.
- Spencer Johnson, another bestselling author, writes the famous *Who Moved My Cheese?* series. This book is so well known it has spawned comic parodies and now feels like a must-read if you lack motivation at work, if only to find out what the fuss is about. The book provides a method for managing change in business, using a parable of mice sniffing after some cheese.

The habits of success method
What is it?
Typified by the famous, bestselling (and also sometimes satirised) *Seven Habits of Highly Effective People*, this approach tends to look at how successful people have achieved their goals in the past and breaks down the approach into traits, rules or habits for others to follow. Malcolm Gladwell's *Outliners* could also fit into this category; so too does writing about the psychology of success or developing a successful mind-set or mental attitude. Writers of these books often include their own stories about how they overcame adversity and developed the successful strategy they now employ. In common with the first method we looked at in this chapter, these kinds of books and programmes sometimes make big claims regarding their effectiveness and can be inflexible about the application of the strategies (you MUST do this if you want to be successful) – to the point that they sometimes seem to achieve cult-like status. If you like the idea of this approach, skim read the book first to make sure it includes at least some practical suggestions that you would find useful. The worst kind in this category tend to be too general, or too dictatorial; the best ones are well-researched and allow us to take specific techniques or suggestions and apply them with flexibility.

Stephen Covey
Covey's work is so influential that many other goal setting or self-help books owe a debt to him. Habit one, "be proactive" surely underpins the adoption of almost any method or technique: as I like to say to my students, you can't get published / get a job / research an essay whilst sitting on the sofa eating crisps. Habit four: "think win / win" has entered popular culture as a self-help idiom. As he has sold millions of copies, if you're interested in this kind of approach, you probably don't need me to describe the book to you! As per the title, Covey unpacks seven habits that he has identified in

successful people across a spectrum of disciplines and walks of life. Simply knowing the chapter headings and what they mean will provide some useful advice when setting goals, and Wikipedia will give you an overview. For example, habit seven "sharpen the saw" involves making sure you take care of yourself. Here, in common with the third method we'll look at, Covey divides "you" into life parts: "physical", "mental", "spiritual" and "social / emotional", and argues that we must recharge and renew each aspect of ourselves. He also has something in common with Julia Cameron's *The Sound of Paper* at this point, despite the fact that the two authors write in such different ways.

Who else writes about it?

- Robert Kelsey. Kelsey describes what he calls "high fear of failure" and how to develop strategies to deal with it in different situations. Part two is about goals. Usefully Kelsey has read lots of self-help and popular psychology and incorporates its advice as he works through the book, giving details in a bibliography.

- Carol S. Dweck. Psychology professor at Stanford and one of the leading writers on the psychology of success, Dweck's most recent book is *Mindset: How You Can Fulfil Your Potential*, and she has also written academic books and articles on the subject. She discusses her work researching people's attitude to success and failure and the difference between a "fixed mindset" and a "growth mindset". Dweck's inspiring work also fits under the mistakes and perseverance category as people with a "growth mindset" use challenges and set backs as a chance to learn. Dweck demonstrates how we can develop such a mindset ourselves.

The life-roles or whole self method

What is it?

This kind of goal setting method involves breaking your life into parts, as you did during chapter three. Sometimes these are referred to as the roles you play in life: parent, daughter, worker etc. You might be encouraged to create your own personal list of roles. Jinny Ditzler takes this approach, for example. Alternatively the roles are provided for you. The author might use specific categories that apply to most people instead of roles, such as health, education, spiritual life, leisure pursuits etc. Some writers give broader categories. For example, Kate Burton structures her book *Live Life, Love Work* (see below) around physical, mental, emotional and purposeful energy and we've already mentioned Covey's divisions. Breaking our lives down like this allows us to do two things:

1) After working out which areas are important to us, we can work out whether we're achieving balance across the different parts of our lives. For example, questions six, seven and eight in Jinny Ditzler *Best Year Yet* give you practical exercises for dealing with this issue.

2) We can identify goals for each category or role.

There are a few problems with this approach. The most obvious one is that all of the areas of our lives intersect and we can't necessarily think about one part of our lives without involving several others. The second is that because most of us play lots of different roles at home and at work, we can easily end up with too many goals. Also, what about goals that are not related to any of your current roles or categories? I might secretly want to be a jazz pianist, but if I've never opened the lid of a piano and don't listen to any jazz, it wouldn't appear on my list of roles or categories. The books I have read of this type tend to acknowledge these problems. If you're taking this approach – and the more specific and detailed it gets, the more useful it becomes – don't forget to use your imagination too.

Kate Burton

Kate Burton is a life coach and NLP practitioner who has several titles to her name. Her book *Live Life, Love Work* has a life-coach-in-your-pocket feel to it and is founded on the principle that we need to consider our whole person when thinking about both work / life balance and about the career that's best for us. She suggests that we need to balance four energies: physical, mental, emotional and purposeful energy and uses these energies to structure the book. Each chapter includes practical exercises and suggestions for improving your health and wellbeing, as well as assertiveness and time management strategies. She also includes strategies gleaned from psychology, particularly to do with why we fall into certain difficult patterns of behaviour and how to stop, and an exercise on identifying personal values.

Who else writes about it?

- Jinny Ditzler. Broken down into ten questions, each one involving practical exercises, Ditzler shows you how to make your next year the 'best year yet' hence the title of her book. I used this method when I was looking for a publisher for my first novel and it worked!

- Brian Mayne. Mayne's work incorporates thinking on the law of attraction and positive thinking, and as such is influenced by new age philosophies. I've put him in this category because if you follow his exercises and draw your goal map (be prepared to draw!) you'll find yourself breaking your life into parts *and* taking small steps back from your main goal. If you like new age approaches, this could be for you. If you don't, you could still get something out of drawing the goal map. Skip to part two and look at the illustrations.

- Tony Buzan. If you like drawing and mapping, try Tony Buzan's work, some of which is listed under 'thinking creatively' in the resources section at the end of this book. Tony Buzan doesn't specifically talk about goal setting from life roles but mind mapping one's goals produces the same kind of effect. (There is a section on goal-setting in *The Mind Map Book*.)

The mistakes and perseverance method
What is it?

This is the idea that one doesn't need inborn talent to succeed, but rather constant practice. The idea came to particular prominence through Malcolm Gladwell's *Outliners*. There have been several books in this field recently, most of them talking about the psychology and philosophy of success and talent – so this isn't really a method as such. We can glean from them a different way of looking at our goals and understand that we need to practise whatever it is we want to achieve and that making mistakes, failing, examining where we went wrong and trying again is a good thing and should be cultivated as an approach rather than avoided. Look into this method if you like thinking and reading about ideas in detail and are fascinated by the philosophy and psychology behind approaches.

The 10,000 hour rule and beyond

Based on research by psychologist Anders Ericsson and made famous by Malcolm Gladwell, this rule states that you need 10,000 hours or ten years to become a virtuoso. Malcolm Gladwell also talks about being in the right place at the right time. One memorable example he gives relates to Bill Gates and the development of personal computing. On the one hand, it seems that a series of chance opportunities allowed Gates the chance to develop his ideas, on the other hand, Gladwell argues, he was both born at the right time, and hardworking enough to take advantage of them.

What's wrong with this approach? It appears to be the polar opposite of Brian Tracey's promise to bring success "faster than you ever dreamed". In other words, knowing about it feels daunting. We have to begin somewhere, and sometimes the first year is just the beginning. In fact, using the strategies I describe in this book, those 10,000 hours break down into lots of small steps. If you have a big ambition or want to become a virtuoso, don't let 10,000 hours scare you. Start with one small thing.

Who else writes about it?

- Oliver Burkeman. *Help: How to Become Slightly Happier and Get a Bit More Done* is a collection of Burkeman's columns from the Guardian Weekend Magazine. This book gives snippets of useful and down-to-earth advice about productivity and becoming happier (as the title suggests) and serves as a review of many different self-help books. Not ostensibly about the importance of mistakes and perseverance or the myth of talent, but its ethos suggests that we need to keep plugging away at the various practical suggestions rather than aiming for some kind of problem-free Nirvana. I've quoted from Burkeman in this book and it's worth knowing that you can read other previously published columns on the Guardian website.

- Tim Harford. Harford is the economist behind *The Undercover Economist*. In his follow up book *Adapt*, he describes how companies and individuals who try flexible and varied approaches – accepting failure as part of that approach – are most likely to find success.

- Matthew Syed. In *Bounce*, this table-tennis champion and sports journalist describes about what he calls the "hidden logic of success", involving hard work and training rather than some kind of inborn talent.

The journey-focused method
What is it?

In this approach one thinks about life as a journey. It often feels spiritual when you read about it (though not always – Shapiro is an exception). This is because many of those who write this way are directly or indirectly inspired by Buddhism. Again this approach is more of a philosophy than a method. Journey-focused writing encourages us to consider the process, to think about the present moment and to practice mindfulness. This isn't so much a strategy for directly working out your goals. Rather you write it out slowly through journaling, or through meditation practice. In fact, some writers in this category advocate living goal-free. Usually the journey is an emotional, creative or spiritual one, but some writers in this category are literally travelling, whether that be around their local area or across continents. Even if you are not interested in a spiritual approach, these kinds of ideas still provide a counterpoint to those who set us striving towards achieving our bigger and better goals at some point in the future.

Goal-free living

Although it sounds like it from the title of Stephen M. Shapiro's book, *Goal-Free Living* isn't exactly anti-goals, but rather anti-blinked stress-inducing goals. Shapiro talks about developing aspirations instead of ridged goal setting. Remember SMART goals from the first example? It's this kind of results-orientated goal-setting he critiques in *Goal-Free Living*. His philosophy reminds me of what Carol S. Dweck calls the "growth mindset". Each encounter and challenge is an opportunity to learn something new. Shapiro structures his books using what he calls the "eight secrets of goal free living" which allows him to elaborate on these ideas. For example, secret one is "use a compass, not a map". (You can read the others on Shapiro's website.) I could have included *Goal-Free Living* in the section on 'habits of success' because the 'secrets' read in a similar way. This approach is very much about enjoying the journey but is the least spiritual of the books reviewed in this section. If you are very concerned and anxious about goal-setting and targets (or you work for a boss who is!) then this will prove a very useful book. If you are already extremely suspicious of rigidly planned SMART-type goal setting, then Shapiro's book might not be radical enough for you.

Who else writes about it?

- Julia Cameron is a writer and artist who is most famous for creating *The Artist's Way* –12-step programme for those who feel drained of creativity – and has helped thousands of people. The practical techniques are useful for anyone who wants to follow a creative path. If you are setting goals in this area, have a look to see if her ideas work for you. Some of my students found the spiritual dimension too overpowering when they experimented with her suggestions but many of them have taken her advice and, for example, keep what she calls "morning pages". *The Sound of Paper,* one of her later books, contains snippets of writing with practical suggestions at the end of each chapter. Look up *The Sound of Paper* if you are interested in writing.

- Tara Brach. Now is a good point to admit that Oliver Burkeman's column in the Guardian 'This Column Will Change Your Life' really did change my life. Because of it, I read *Radical Acceptance* by Tara Brach. Brach is a Buddhist practitioner who, through her meditation CDs, website and books, gives a unique take on applying mindfulness to every moment. This is an inspirational book and a useful antidote to a life full of planning and struggling for success.

- Jack Kornfield. If you are attracted to the spiritual side of these ideas, look into Jack Kornfield's books. Kornfield is a major influence on Tara Brach and his work is probably more about goal-free living than Shapiro's!

Commonalities and concluding thoughts
Comparing the approaches

We could place these books about goal-setting and their attitude to it on a continuum. Brian Tracey's direct approach which leads to thorough planning, and very specific measurable, result-oriented goals would be at one end, with some of the other books about selling and performance at work, probably followed by the habits of success methods. The journey-focused writers would be at the other end: aspirations are encouraged, but here the approach is all about process, being OK now, being mindful of the present moment. What I've called the 'life roles or whole-self method' and the 'mistakes and perseverance method' would feature somewhere in the middle. Having said that, one striking thing about these methods is that each has a structure, rules, guidelines, sometimes highly directed, sometimes merely suggested, but at the same time the *content* of the goals remains up to the reader.

Instead of our continuum, we could let the differences between the approaches go into soft focus for a second and look at the wisdom we can glean from an overview:

- If you're going to have goals, specificity is a good idea.
- Knowing what your personal values are is crucial to all of these approaches.
- Whatever you do, don't be so focused on the results of your plan that you forget about either i) the process of getting there ii) being happy in each moment.
- Making mistakes, facing challenges, and our attitude to failures are all crucial to your happiness.
- Effort is required. Instant results aren't a good thing.

- Thinking about the whole of your life and the different roles you play will stop you from becoming super-focused on one area.

What next?

Personally I've found Jinny Ditzler and Tara Brach inspiring so can highly recommend their work. That said, I hope I've given you enough information to decide for yourself whether you would like to follow up any of these leads.

Key points

In this chapter we've covered:

1. What is the productivity, work or sales method?
    - Brian Tracey's *Goals!*
    - Who else writes about it?
        - o Zig Ziglar
        - o Spencer Johnson
2. What is the habits of success method?
    - Stephen Covey's Seven Habits
    - Who else writes about the habits of success method?
        - o Robert Kelsey
        - o Carol S. Dweck
3. What is the life-roles or whole self method?
    - Kate Burton's *Live Life, Love Work*
    - Who else writes about the life-roles or whole self method?
        - o Jinny Ditzler
        - o See also: Brian Mayne and Tony Buzan
4. What is the mistakes and perseverance method?
    - Malcolm Gladwell: The 10,000 hour rule and beyond
    - Who else writes about the mistakes and perseverance method?

- o Oliver Burkeman
- o Tim Harford
- o Matthew Syed

5. What is the journey-focused method?
   - Stephen M. Shapiro's *Goal-free living*
   - Who else writes about journey-focused method?
     - o Julia Cameron
     - o Tara Brach
     - o Jack Kornfield

6. Commonalities and concluding thoughts

****

Chapter 8: Motivation. What Is It? Do You Need It?

About this chapter

In this chapter, we start by trying to define motivation. Is it an abstract concept, an emotion, something busy people have, something other people have, or something everyone has? Next you're given some practical suggestions for developing more motivation, using the small steps method. The rest of this chapter examines the different contradictions that arise when we try to pin down exactly what motivation is. Because motivation is so elusive, each section of this chapter contradicts the last somehow! I've given you lots of small steps exercises along the way so you can work out what motivation means to you.

What is motivation?
An abstract concept
The trouble with motivation is that it's an abstract concept. No one really knows what it is or where it comes from. It's easy to imagine that motivation is a special force that exists either inside us or, elusively, 'out there' somewhere - or that it's an emotion that makes us feel ready to achieve whatever we want to achieve.

So is motivation an emotion?
Feelings of commitment and equanimity come from absence of guilt and tend to happen when we only need to focus on one task at a time. Guilt, boredom or frustration are all symptoms of the same problem. They are signs that you want or need to do something else, *not* that the task you're doing is uninteresting or unnecessary.

It's possible to do absolutely nothing and feel fine. According to Tara Brach who I reviewed in chapter seven, simply stopping, acknowledging and naming out loud – or writing down - what you want or need to do can help.

But aren't busy people more motivated?

If you find that busyness is a motivating force, it's likely that, because you're busy, you've allocated the task a timeslot and that a side-effect of your busyness is at least partial efficiency. You're getting enough done to allow yourself to feel motivated.

If we think about it rationally, motivation is only a set of circumstances which, at the same time as providing us with the time and space to do whatever it is, and removing distractions, also make us feel committed and at ease. Given our busy lives, it's going to be a very happy coincidence if all of these circumstances and feelings happen at once.

Other people have it (Do they really?)

Often we compare ourselves to others and remember from chapter six that happiness has been strongly linked to such comparisons. We assume that everyone around us is motivated and feel demotivated ourselves. Fundamental attribution error is a term from psychology that is useful to apply here. Fundamental attribution error means that we assume, wrongly, that someone's behaviour is a result of an inner 'fundamental' trait. A classmate is always late, we assume he or she is a late person. We're late, we blame it on our circumstances: the traffic was bad, the bus drivers were on strike. Arguably *every* action is a result of a particular set of circumstances or contexts rather than fundamental traits. We can leave that one to the psychologists, but when you see someone out jogging – looking motivated to keep fit – you don't know his or her circumstances. He or she is not necessarily or even probably 'fundamentally' motivated any more than you are. It follows that if we change our circumstances in just a small way – ask a friend to go jogging with us, join an NHS Stop Smoking Group – we don't need to be fundamentally motivated anyhow.

Everybody has it (Why else do you get out of bed?)
Thinking rationally again – which isn't easy to do when you're trying to muster up some motivation – everybody must have some kind of motivation. You're motivated enough to read these words. We're motivated enough to meet our basic physical needs. *Something* is making you do what you do all day, whether that's sitting on the sofa playing computer games and eating crisps, or going to work and coming home again. Far from being elusive, that motivational force is something we can harness.

The Motivation Game: a day in the life.
Here's a small step you can take. Try playing the motivation game. Take one day in your life. Write down what you did. Make a list of all the key activities. Write down the reason you did each thing. We're not after deep reasons this time. Write down what made you do each activity in that particular moment in time. The motivation game proves that, somehow, we're already motivating ourselves. One thing that comes up again and again in the motivation game is habit. Why did you do X? *Because I always do X on a Monday afternoon.*

How to develop more motivation
Motivation and small steps
So given that we don't really know what motivation is, how on earth do you get motivated to achieve your goals? This is a conundrum that has filled many pages of self-help books. Motivation may not arrive until you start doing it. Following the methods in this book, take some small steps. Do these small,

manageable steps daily and the motivation will follow. In this section you'll find some more motivation tips:

Make it a habit

We perform tasks habitually. This is a good thing. It would be a difficult life if we had to think carefully through the process of making a coffee or driving a car each time we did it. How to make the habit habit work for you:

- Try to become more aware of your regular daily routines. Could you make your small steps habitual somehow? Form positive habits. I decided to go to an exercise class every week. I don't think about it as I walk to the class. I just turn up. Afterwards I'm glad I took the class. It is habitual: every Monday morning I go to my exercise class.

- Are you habitually doing anything that is sapping your motivation? For example, the daily commute often saps our energy. Could you change the way you get to work? Could you work from home?

Picture your higher motivations

Higher motivations are the people and things that inspire you to achieve your goals, the people you love above anything else and the things you hold dear. For example, your children and your grandchildren or your desire to be fit into your old age or your commitment to caring for our planet.

If you've been working through the exercises in this part of the book, you should know by now what you want to achieve. You know your smaller goals and you know your seemingly impossible dreams. Try this:

- Stop for a moment and look back over the goals you've set yourself.

- Can you specifically name your higher motivations?

It's often when we come face-to-face with a specific example of a higher motivation that it becomes extremely powerful. This can be as simple as watching a grandchild playing on a beach. To go someway towards replicating this effect, keep a picture with you, a picture that reminds you of your higher motivations. It can be a physical picture or a detailed mental one.

Discover your values

In chapter six, we heard briefly from a BBC interview with Dr Happiness, Ed Diener, who said that having goals that attune with our *values* is important for happiness. Values infuse everything we do. They tend to be general guiding principles, rather than specific rules. Here are three ways to discover your values.

1. Your higher motivations will be underpinned by your values. Write down your higher motivation and work out the *belief* behind it. For example:

Higher motivation	Value
I am motivated by...	*I believe in...*
My children and grandchildren grandchildren	Parenting and family
My desire to be fit into my old age	Health and wellbeing
My commitment to caring for the planet	Environment and community

2. Sometimes it's hard to know what your values are until they are challenged. Try thinking about work-based or social

scenarios that made you uncomfortable and ask yourself *why*.

3. Imagine the ideal you. How you are on your best days? How you would like other people to see you? Turn the ideal you into a list of single word descriptions. For example: fashionable, clever, witty, kind, loving, fair, sporty, fun, laid-back. Put down as many as you can, then circle your top three. Based on your list, what are your values?

Once you know what they are, go through the life parts you figured out in chapter three. Ask yourself if there any parts of your life which aren't consistent with your values.

Solve your small wants

Your higher motivations are probably different from your daily motivations. Some commentators have called these 'big wants' and 'small wants.' (For example, Jinny Ditzler talks about big and little wants in her book *Best Year Yet.*) Using the example of my exercise class again, my higher motivation – or my 'big want' – is the idea of living a fit and healthy life. When I wake up early on Monday morning, my 'small want' is to go back to sleep. The greater the disparity between your big wants and small wants, the more frustrated you'll feel. Sometimes the key to motivation is to *solve the small wants.* If I went to bed a hour earlier on Sunday night, perhaps I wouldn't want to go back to sleep quite so much on Monday morning. 'Small wants' might include:

- Enough sleep
- An adequate space to work
- Encouragement from a partner or friend – a big help in getting me to my exercise class!

- An end to distractions and interruptions – those you can control like email and those you can't like noisy neighbours

Get rid of the niggles: a practical exercise
Write down every niggle: anything that annoys you, interrupts you, frustrates you or prevents you from doing what you want to do, goal related or otherwise. Spend some time recording these things in your notebook. Solving these 'small wants' is an uplifting experience. You might find that you didn't need motivation, you needed to sort out the niggles.

When small wants aren't so small
A defining feature of 'small wants' is that they often go unidentified. When you begin to pin them down you might find they are part of a bigger problem – in other words they are not small at all. For example 'enough sleep' features on the list of small wants above. Wanting to get back under the duvet instead of getting up to exercise doesn't seem so serious, but getting enough sleep is crucial for our health and vitality – are any of your small wants symptoms of a bigger problem? If so, have a go at working out some related small steps today, using the earlier chapters of this book.

What motivates you to do what you do now?
Look back at the results of the Motivation Game. You are already motivated to do these things. Can you simply change the activity – or most likely the habitual behaviour – to something more in line with your goals?

Lack motivation? It's a sign!
If you think you lack motivation, if you feel bored, guilty or frustrated, it's *a sign that something needs to change.* Reformulate your thinking, and see your lack of motivation as a signal to do

something different. Now you can take some action, just one small step. You might need to identify your 'small wants' and solve them first. Ironically you'll have used your apparent lack of motivation to kick start the process. The small steps method is so effective because it focuses on taking one small step after another. Do one small thing towards changing your circumstances today.

You don't need motivation
Do it anyway
Oliver Burkeman sums up this approach to motivation as follows: "one single-sentence piece of fridge-magnet advice has helped vastly more [...] than everything else combined: Don't wait until you feel like doing something."

Have you tripped over a motivation stumbling block?
You've tripped over a motivation stumbling block, if, as Oliver Burkeman points out, you wait until you feel motivated or inspired before doing something. This problem is something of a vicious circle: you'll end up getting stuck doing the same old thing, which makes it less likely you'll feel like it.

You may also have tripped over a motivation stumbling block if you start a task but don't see it through because you don't feel motivated. In this case, we typically feel enthusiastic about *starting* a project and excited about the *end result*, whether it's a weight-loss programme, or learning to speak Mandarin, but get frustrated by the *middle* of a project.

Of course, that's not the same as realising you're not fit enough, or that the activity is too dangerous, or that the goal isn't for you after all. Remember the alcoholic's prayer? This is when you need the 'wisdom to know the difference'. If you're part way through a project and feel like giving up, go back and review your goals. If you're still in doubt, ask someone who knows you well whether you should keep going.

If you don't feel motivated, do it anyway. Forget about what motivation is and how you develop it. You don't need it. Take one small step instead, and another and another. You can take small steps without motivation. As long as you are moving towards your goals, and you've thought them through in advance, how positive you feel about the individual steps doesn't matter. Just as I try not to think about exercising as I walk to my class across the park in the morning, get on with it and don't analyse it. Remember to make the steps small and specific.

Turn up
This is small steps principle number 8. Taking small steps means *turning up*. After I've turned up at my exercise class it would be embarrassing to walk out again. Fiction writers call this technique 'turning up at the page'. In other words, giving yourself the space and time to write, then sitting down to write and letting yourself off the hook. We turn up at the page, and then see what happens. You can apply the same idea to any goal you want to achieve. Give yourself adequate time and space to do it. Then turn up. Don't attempt to motivate yourself or analyse why you are there. If this is too difficult on your own, find a class to turn up to or turn up to your goal with a friend.

Motivation doesn't exist!
Why we need structure (and confuse structure for motivation)
It's possible that motivation doesn't really exist at all. It's just another word for structure, perseverance or habit. Take structure for instance. We thrive on it. From your morning routine, to the meeting schedule at work, to the train timetable on the way home, to the babysitting rota, we use structure to make sense of our day-

to-day lives. Even if we think of ourselves as easy-going and flexible, we still have our own particular way of getting from breakfast to bed time. What happens when we try to add something new? It disrupts the existing structure. We often confuse the unease this causes for lack of motivation. We can also confuse the security we get from structuring our lives in a particular way with motivation. The (difficult) trick is to use the structure of our lives and build in time for the things we really want to achieve. By the way, this is why vague goals like 'I'll write my memoir one day' or 'I'll learn to scuba dive when I have some free time' don't work. Although as you saw in the previous chapter, Stephen M. Shapiro might not agree with me!

Use routine

Create a routine for the week and a routine for your day. Make it flexible. Discuss it with your partner or a friend. Stick it up somewhere you can see it. My early morning exercise class has become a habit because my partner looks after our son while I go to it. It's part of our routine. What can you incorporate into your daily and weekly routine? Don't underestimate this tool: it replaces motivation with habit very quickly.

Structure 101

Structure isn't only about routine: our homes have a structure, our filing has a structure, our kitchen cupboards have a structure. Are the pans you need for cooking stuck on a shelf somewhere hard to reach? You may not have thought about it, you just curse to yourself every time you reach for the pans: but you are much more likely to be motivated to cook healthy meals instead of buying TV Dinners if those pans are within easy reach. You might actually be putting on weight because your pans are in an awkward cupboard! Make the structures in your life work for you.

Incorporate and swap

So we know that habit is a key motivator in what we do already on a day-to-day basis. Extend your record of what you do every day. Keep it going for a week. Where do you have space to incorporate a key goal-related activity? Which activities could you swap for something else to make them more goal-oriented?

The tyranny of 'instant results'

Certain parts of modern culture encourage us to expect instant results. Internet search engines, instant celebrities created by reality shows, skin care products that are supposed to work in just a few seconds, diets that claim to get you slim in a week, lotteries that promise millions in prize money instantly. It's possible to become so tuned into the expectation of instant gratification that we associate it with the value and quality of an experience or achievement.

Listen to the masters

Anyone who has become a master of a discipline - a master craftsman, an accomplished musician, a sculptor with many year's experience, an Olympic athlete, a scientist or a medical pioneer who has spent many hours in training - will tell you that the reverse is true. Value and quality come from spending many hours, days, weeks and years perfecting and practising a skill. It's not only the end result that these masters of their craft, trade or science value. Listen to one of them being interviewed and more likely than not they'll say that although it was hard, and involved sacrifices, the process was as important as the end result. We're all familiar with this idea because we've all spent many hours, days, weeks and years perfecting and practising particular skills, whether we happen to be leading violinists or scientists or not. These are the ordinary every day skills that we don't think twice about.

Mistakes / practice / repetition

I pointed out in chapter four that humans learn by making mistakes. We make a mistake, practise and repeat. We're hardwired to learn like this because of the way human beings evolved to use tools and to communicate with one another. The expectation of instant gratification can exacerbate any motivation stumbling block and make us lose enthusiasm for a project as soon as it seems hard.

The trouble is, many people feel like giving up after the first mistake. We feel deflated. We lose enthusiasm. But we can't succeed unless we make mistakes. Therefore your attitude to the process of mistakes / practice / repetition could govern your ability to succeed. We've already said that successful people have a different attitude to failure from everyone else. They see each knockback as a lesson. They deliberately set things in motion knowing that some approaches will fail but at least one will succeed. (Look into Carol Dweck's work if you like this idea.)

This is why small steps principles 6 and 7 are so important. Do them and your attitude and motivation levels don't matter so much. Remember:

- Small steps don't necessarily go in a straight line.
- Take lots of small steps, especially at the beginning.

Mistakes / practice / repetition exercise:

This exercise is designed to get you thinking about how one masters a skill.

1. Take one of the skills you identified in the first chapter under '*Do you need a goal?*' Something you can do well. Something you've known how to do for a long time. Write down how you acquired the skill.
2. Go out and learn something new. Take a day or a couple of evenings to learn the beginnings of it. Ideally ask someone

who is already an expert to teach you the skill. Write down how you acquired the skill.

3. Teach someone a skill. Write down how they acquired the skill.

Key motivation blind-spots
Introducing the common motivation blind-spots
Here are common goals that are notorious for motivation stumbling blocks. We tend to assume that we need to get motivated *before* we do each of these things while at the same time doing them or not doing them could have a major influence on our lives. The small steps suggested here are just that: suggestions. If these happen to be your personal goals, then go through the goal setting process outlined in the opening chapters of the book. All of these small steps demonstrate another crucial part of the small steps method, summed up by principle number 4. After you've taken one small step, take another small step *even if the first step leaves you feeling demotivated, defeated or down-in-the-dumps*. Remember that when you plan your small steps they need to be as specific as possible.

Quit smoking
Don't wait for the will power. Take a small step today. Stop by the health centre on the way to the shops to join a Stop Smoking group, get a book from the library on the way home from work, or make an appointment to see your doctor. Now plan your next small step.

Exercise regularly
Don't wait until you feel like it. Take a small step. Go for a swim instead of watching TV tonight. Walk to work tomorrow morning. Do some gardening this weekend. Now plan your next small step.
Eat healthily

Eating unhealthily can cause blood sugar levels to seesaw, making it likely that we'll crave more unhealthy foods *and* that our moods will be affected. In other words, *you won't ever feel like it* if you carry on eating unhealthily. Take a small step. This evening, look online for an article or a recipe book that explains how foods affect your moods. Now plan your next small step.

Creative activities

There's something about dancing, singing, painting, writing, or expressing yourself creatively that forces you to think and feel in a different way. Try it now. Put your favourite music on and move around the room to it. Or sing your favourite song as loud as you dare. Again, waiting for inspiration is a misnomer. Inspiration comes from doing it. Take a small step. Put aside one hour this week to do something creative that you've always wanted to try. Know nothing about it? Remember how we added the word 'research' earlier to create small steps? You could put aside one hour this week to research whatever it is and to create some small steps for yourself.

I've always wanted to…(really?)

Sometimes we hold on to ambitions that don't really fit any more. Look over the goals you've set for yourself, the skills you've identified and the values you hold. Is this goal – the thing you've always wanted to do - really worth holding onto? Why haven't you ever done it? Try to get down to the specific reasons. Take a small step. Do one thing this week towards realising this ambition. Or if it no longer suits you, let it go. Now plan your next small step.

No need to get motivated

Five practical exercises to help you get over a motivation stumbling block:

- Your habits: over a week write down what you do habitually.
- Your key times: over a week write down your key stress points and record moments when you had time spare.
- Your small irritations: over a week record any small things that annoy you. Try go get down as many niggles as possible.
- Your space: take a weekend (or longer of you need it) to make sure the space you live and work in is as easy to use as possible.
- Your stuff: take a weekend (or longer of you need it) to make sure the stuff around you is not only consummate with your values, but also isn't holding you back. The stuff around you needs to support you.

Key points
In this chapter we've covered:

1. What is motivation? An abstract concept, an emotion, something busy people have, other people have, or everyone has?
2. How to develop more motivation, including: make it a habit, picture your higher motivations, discover your values, and solve your small wants.
3. You don't need motivation, including: do it anyway, turn up, incorporate and swap, and use routine.
4. Motivation doesn't exist, including: why we need structure, the tyranny of 'instant results', listen to the masters, and mistakes / practice / repetition
5. Key motivation blind-spots: quit smoking, exercise regularly, eat healthily, creative activities, and I've always wanted to.

Part 2: Time management

Chapter 9: Small Steps to Time Management.

About this chapter
This chapter introduces the second section of the book, which is all about small steps time management. I start by telling you more about what's included. Then I'll ask you to begin to think about time management and what it means. The chapter finishes with another look at the 10 principles of the small steps method with an indication of how they apply to this section, plus a quick review of some popular time management methods. It's worth reiterating that in this section you should pick only the exercises you feel are relevant to your situation and that some are repeated and developed to help you practise particular techniques.

Small steps time management: an introduction
What is time management?
The term 'time management' suggests that we can organise and control the way we use time. If you're interested in it, then there must be some periods of time in your life that you want to organise better. Time management is also big business with plenty of self-help books and business resources available on the subject. The term 'time management' also suggests that there's need for some kind of solution and that if only we could find out what it is, our organisational problems would be over! But no time management system can offer a magic wand. In order to introduce something new into our lives, we've either got to become more efficient (which isn't always possible) or stop doing something else, or both. The good news is that in order to achieve your goals you *don't* have to

schedule every minute of everyday! There are some small and easy steps you can take to become more organised.

Two things you can't forget about time management

1. You can't forget your context – or your big picture - when you're thinking about time management. Your context – the environment, people, spaces, resources and things that surround you – will either help or hinder you in the task you've set yourself. In turn, allowing for your context means you manage time effectively. More on the big picture in the next chapter.

2. Some things take time. Forget about instant results. To watch this in action, take a small step today and *plant something*. Go to a garden shop or call on a gardening friend. Put some bulbs down. Plant some seedlings. More on this below under 'garden time'.

What is small steps time management?

This section sets out the small steps approach to time management. When applying the ideas you'll find here, work with the goals you set in the previous section. In chapter ten, we look at some examples of small steps time management in action and discover some time management basics and some tips for getting more specific. In chapter eleven, you'll analyse the way you use time, looking at your current rhythms and peaks and troughs. Then in chapters twelve to fourteen we go on to the core of small steps time management:

-   set it up, break it down, make it easy,
-   make it count, keep it balanced, think whole picture and
-   balanced planning

Finally in chapters fifteen and sixteen, you'll look at some small adjustments you can incorporate and small tools you can use to make time work for your goals, whatever they are.

Why is time management important when you're setting goals?

- Without time management, goals become aspirational things, dreams that we want to achieve one day, things that we hope will happen by chance.
- Without time management, we may not be sure how long it will take us to achieve our goals or where the end point lies.
- Without time management, we might know what the steps are – and even try multiple small steps to get us started – but we never make progress.
- Without time management, we don't necessarily know whether we want to achieve our goals. Ironically, it's not until they stop being dreams and we make them part of our routine and our lives that we discover the value of our goals.
- Without time management, we won't what it will cost us. We won't know what the commitment means. Put simply, in order to do one thing, we have to *not* do something else or we have to become more efficient.

When a problem isn't a problem (when it's about time)

To me this is a fundamental aspect of successful time management and one which is often ignored by self-help books. In chapter four, I mentioned a student who was trying to write to the sound of her neighbours renovating their house. She thought she had writer's block. Her immediate problem was that she needed to find somewhere quiet to write, but when we delved a little deeper the issue was actually about turning up – small steps principle number 8. And turning up requires two things: *space and time.*

Turning up requires space, and *appropriate space* at that. In other words, this student needed somewhere peaceful. As we've

111

discovered, we also need the right equipment. We need somewhere *to turn up to*.

Garden time

Turning up requires time. Yes, we need a block of time when we are not required to do anything else, but also we need time in the way a garden needs time. You need to tend and care for a garden over years in order to take pleasure in seeing it grow and mature. Apply this to other tasks and projects in our lives and we could call it 'garden time'. This student needed to take the time to write one page and then another page and then another, not just because the actual process of writing takes a block of time to accomplish, but because the project needs to mature and grow. Remember what we said earlier about instant gratification? It can play havoc with time management. It can stop us doing anything that will require garden time.

So now's the time to start digging! When you're creating a garden from scratch it helps to come up with some small steps and not to be overawed by the hugeness of the project. Once you've created your plan, you're going to have to get down and dig at some point.

In a way, the student who thought she had writer's block didn't have a problem at all. She needed find an appropriate space and *to give it time*. She wasn't going to be able to write a novel in a week. Ironically we can get so hung up (often subconsciously) on the issue of substantial time commitment, that we don't do anything at all. If we take it seriously, the small steps method solves this issue. Turn up, write a page. Turn up, do the exercise class. Turn up, buy some fresh vegetables. Whatever it is, take small steps and give it some garden time. Once you've realised this, you can let go of the amount of time it will take, and simply turn up regularly.

The 10 small steps principles revisited

The small steps method is about taking a task and breaking it down into small steps – this applies to time management too. Below I've repeated the 10 small steps principles, and I've pointed out in italics how you can use them to get to grips with time management. The rest of this section expands on these themes, incorporating advice about goals along the way.

1. Small steps are small. Break down a task until you get to something you could easily achieve today. *Once you've broken down a task like this, you can easily add the steps to your schedule.*

2. Small steps are specific and concrete. Make the small steps as down-to-earth and measurable as possible, if this is an approach you like. *You can give yourself short deadlines. You'll know when you've done it!*

3. Small steps don't cost a fortune. Do as many free steps as possible first. Financing a project can also be broken down into small steps. *Schedule the free steps first.*

4. Small steps are just like footsteps: Take one small step and take another small step after it. Keep taking small steps. *Because they're small, you can invent small steps to do everyday and fit them around your routine.*

5. Small steps are just small steps. They don't rely on luck, on other people, or on results. *This kind of time management is supposed to be stress-free not stress-full. Break it down, schedule it, then (try to) let go of the results.*

6. Small steps don't necessarily go in a straight line. One action doesn't have to lead directly to the next, as long as they all relate back to the task. *Once you know what the small steps are, you can use small chunks of time or you can cluster tasks together.*

7. Take lots of small steps, especially at the beginning. *You've got your day-to-day, week-by-week, month-by-month*

routines; you've got your small steps. Analyse your peaks and troughs so you know when to begin a project.

8. Turn up. Small steps require you to get off the sofa. *Give yourself the time and the space to do what you want to do.*

9. Once you've prepared, you can do small steps without even thinking about it. *Schedule some preparation time and some review time. The rest of the time, take the small step – don't analyse.*

10. Small steps deserve to be appreciated. Pause at regular intervals to acknowledge your progress and to keep in check. Keep some kind of record in a notebook or journal, on a computer or on your blog. *Use your notebook to look in detail at how you use your time and to evaluate after the event.*

A review of time-management methods

I haven't included a whole chapter reviewing existing time management methods, but have instead peppered those I've found useful throughout the whole of this book or included them in the resources section. Those I've found most useful include:

- David Allen's *Getting Things Done*. To follow David Allen's advice, start by piling up everything you need to do and go through it. Do anything that can be done in 2 minutes. Action everything else. There's much more detail in his book, of course. I recommend reading it if you are snowed under, or if managing information is as important as managing your time. 43 folders is a blog dedicated to creative time management, and includes more on David Allen's approach.

- Read the sections on 'How to Rule the Office' and 'How to Get More Done' in Oliver Burkeman's *Help!* for some practical and very down-to-earth time-management tips.

- The Pomodoro Technique, created by Francesco Cirillo. It will help you to know about the Pomodoro Technique as you work through this section. You can download the book and find out more about it for free on the Pomodoro website. In this technique, one uses a kitchen timer to time 25 minute bursts of activity, with no interruptions, followed by a five minute break. It's called the Pomodoro Technique because the kitchen timer used by Cirillo is shaped like a tomato (or Pomodoro in Italian).

- *Organise Yourself.* Ronni Eisenberg's book contains straight-forward, sensible and down-to-earth suggestions for organising your life.

- Mark Forster is a well-known author on time management. His bestselling books *Get Everything Done and Still Have Time to Play* and *Do It Tomorrow* contain lots of tips for becoming more efficient and demonstrate his developing systems for organising and prioritising your tasks. The current system is called *final version* – a way of selecting tasks from a to do list - and you can find out about it on Forster's website.

- Merlin Mann's blog *43 Folders* is an innovative way to find out more about how to manage your time so you can live a creative life.

Key points

In this chapter we've covered:

1. What is time management? And what is small steps time management?
2. Why is time management important when you're setting goals?
3. When a problem isn't a problem (when it's about time)
4. The 10 small steps principles, and how you can used them to get to grips with time management.
5. A review of some existing time-management methods

****

Chapter 10: Small Steps Time Management In Action

About this chapter

In this chapter we look at two goal-setters, Mrs Brown and Mr Green, and two different kinds of goal. Then I go over some time management basics, the things you need to get to grips with in order to handle any kind of project or task where time management is important. We'll go onto some specifics, again using Mrs Brown and Mr Green as examples, and finish with some practical exercises, where you get to practise 'breaking it down' and working out a timeframe.

When you're applying the ideas in this chapter to your own goals, remember to break the task or project down into small steps until you get to something you could achieve today. If you find it's impossible to create small steps because you don't know enough about it yet, create a research task as you did in the first section and break *that* down into small steps. Remember that asking for advice is a kind of research.

Time management examples

When time management is important

It isn't necessary to manage every aspect of our lives with minute-by-minute precision. That kind of approach sounds hard to me – and also anxiety-inducing and guilt-ridden. There are some situations where managing your time successfully is important and these situations come up when we are hoping to achieve our goals *and* get on with our day-to-day lives. (Look into Stephen M.

Shapiro's "eight secrets of goal-free living" for more on this idea.) Let's look at a couple of examples where time management is important: studying and writing a novel.

Introducing Mrs Brown and Mr Green

Let's imagine Mrs Brown has made it her goal to pursue a particular career and for the career she has in mind, she needs to study at university level. In a way, her degree course is a separate goal, though it will help if she treats it as an overlapping goal and keeps her career aims in mind as she pursues it. She has applied and is about to start.

Let's imagine a second person, we'll call him Mr Green, has decided to write a novel. He's always loved reading. He's done a couple of short courses in Creative Writing and feels ready to start.

Time management basics

Consider the time constraints

On a course of study you'll be given a particular amount of study to do within a certain timeframe. Inside that timeframe there will be constraints such as essay deadlines and exams, term dates and vacations. Mrs Brown needs to consider what time commitment is expected of her.

When it comes to writing his first novel, it's likely Mr Green has no particular time limit in mind. There's no pressure to finish. In other words the process hasn't been structured for him. He needs to consider his own time constraints and decide how much time to commit each week.

Consider resources and information

For Mrs Brown, the reading materials and course information are especially important. It's likely she'll been given lots of information at different stages, which is a process she needs to manage by keeping records. For example, student handbooks, reading lists and assessment requirements may be given out in advance or at the start of term or posted online. Without time management, it's likely she'll run scared from one deadline to the next, not covering enough of the course materials along the way and therefore not doing as well as she could have done. In other words, poor time management could actually affect her degree classification.

There are two types of resources and information Mr Green needs to consider. Firstly, research he does into the themes he's writing about. Secondly, any information about the writing community, in his local area and further afield.

Both goal-setters need to be proactive about resources and information: Mrs Brown has to manage the information she's given about her course (possibly too much of it!) and be proactive about filling any gaps - whereas Mr Green's only option is to go out and find it himself.

Consider time and space

Both our fictional goal-setters need to make sure they have an *appropriate* space to work in. It's pretty obvious that dreaming about his book will put his imagination to work but won't get words down on the page: Mr Green needs to put aside some regular time to work on his book. Equally, Mrs Brown needs to be proactive about putting aside time to study and about learning some study skills. This isn't as obvious as it seems. Some students wait for their tutor's say-so, or only see class time as important. At degree-level, setting aside your own study time is crucial. University gives you the opportunity and structure to study a subject you are interested in. Unlike school and college, a lot of this studying is done on your own, especially if you are an arts student.

Consider the big picture

Both Mrs Brown and Mr Green need to consider their context: the people and things around them that will affect their studies: their family, their job if they have one, their accommodation needs, relationship, social life, and anyone they are caring for. In my experience, many students have a part-time job and many are caring for a family member. Almost all writers do a job alongside their writing.

The big picture has such an impact on how we manage our time that Mrs Brown and Mr Green can't compartmentalise too much in the planning stages. Remember that in order to dedicate time to something you must stop doing something else or become more efficient. Now this might be something unimportant, like time spent lying on the sofa doing nothing, but it's likely both goal-setters will have to make sacrifices and also that Mr Green will have a harder job explaining this to his family and friends, just because Mrs Brown's goal has an external structure to it.

Ask yourself: does it come with an existing structure?

With any task, think about whether it comes with some kind of existing externally-imposed structure – like a course, programme, work project, artistic production – in which case make sure you are still *proactive* in your approach: don't just wait for it to happen to you! Or do you need to create a self-imposed time management structure? What challenges does that present? If you know you work better with an external or self-imposed structure, consider changing the approach you're taking to play to your strengths. For example, signing up to an exercise class works better for me than using an exercise DVD at home. Whereas although I finished my first novel during an MA in Creative Writing, I now prefer to impose my own structure when I'm writing.

Two different approaches with common themes

We have two different kinds of goals here, and it looks like they require different approaches to time management. Mrs Brown's goal comes with an existing externally-imposed structure: but to get the most out of her course she still needs to be proactive about achieving her goal. She can't just turn up at class without preparation. Mr Green's goal relies on a self-imposed time management structure: the danger for him is that without an external structure, with no-one to answer to in the initial stages, it will be easy to skip writing sessions. By the way, this is one reason why joining a writing group can help.

Key considerations for everyone

Even though these two goals appear to require different approaches, we see some common themes emerging and in fact we can apply them to any task that requires successful time management. These are the time management basics. If you like, they're the foundation for any other tip or technique you want to use. We *always* need to consider:

- any time constraints
- resources and information
- time and space
- the big picture
- whether it comes with its own structure

Time management specifics

Prepare

Mrs Brown can get as much information in advance as possible: key dates and deadlines, assessment requirements, tutor's office location and contact details and reading lists. Mr Green can also furnish himself with information by reading books and magazines on writing and by joining a writing group. He can prepare himself for his novel-writing project practically too.

121

Action – take some small steps

Start taking small steps as soon as you can. Mrs Brown could read through her reading list in advance. When I wrote my first novel I took one afternoon off a week. This amounted to two hours work by the time I got home, but it got me started – and created a timetable for me.

Create a Master Plan

Once Mrs Brown has an idea of how her first year as a student will pan out, she can create a Master Plan. Mr Green can also plan his year from scratch this way. A Master Plan could be a Mind Map or a chart or table or a plan of the year on a large sheet of paper. **On the website you can download a bonus bit where I talk you through my method for writing a Small Steps Master Plan as well as a template for creating one.** Once you've done your Master Plan, you can transpose it to a printed year planner, calendar, diary or hand-held device if you need to. You'll need your Master Plan for one of the exercises in the next chapter.

Kick out any time-consuming habits

This is where Mrs Brown and Mr Green need to look at their current lives and ask: is there anything I'm doing that I could stop doing? This tends to be a habit that isn't very important. If they leave out this step, and still pursue their goal, they'll find themselves not doing something by default, and it could turn out to be something important like time with family. Chapter fourteen on balanced planning will help with this one.

Ask for advice

Advice isn't the same as information, and it matters who gives it. Seek out an expert – not necessarily a professional expert. You could simply ask someone who has trodden this way before. Advice getting is especially important if you don't know what to expect. Ask someone in the know about planning your time.

Schedule
Both Mrs Brown and Mr Green can block out sessions in their diaries each week to do their work. Then they can concentrate on turning up to each session. A session is either a morning, afternoon or evening, with breaks built in.

Mrs Brown can use the structure that exists at her university – the course structure, the tutors, the environment, the library, any study skills sessions – to make progress. She'll also need to add some of her own independent study sessions, about one or two a day if she is studying fulltime.

Mr Green needs to create his own schedule. When I'm writing it helps me to act as if I'm going to work and turn up at the library, 9 – 5, with an hour for lunch. Most writers consider time constraints to be a good thing. For example, Mr Green can schedule his own deadlines, such as *send three chapters to an agent in January* or *enter a short story competition in November.*

They can both set small tasks to complete at the beginning of each week. *I will read X article on Wednesday afternoon / I will edit chapter 3 on Wednesday afternoon* for example.

Peeks and troughs
With all kinds of studying there will be peeks and troughs in terms of pressure and deadlines. (More on this in the next chapter.) Mrs Brown can use time she *won't* be seeing tutors or attending class – called 'non-contact time' - to read or study. They will both need to plan around the peeks and troughs in their other commitments over the year. A year planner or calendar will help you to consider the

peaks and troughs of your year, including family commitments, deadlines, work, childcare, social occasions and vacations.

Avoid distractions

This is a tough one when there are so many things competing for our attention. If you prepare well, and schedule well, you can go a long way to avoiding this problem before it happens. Take a note of the things that distract you and – if they are important – schedule some time for them. Self-denial doesn't usually work. Make sure you've done the niggles exercise in chapter eight.

Delays happen

Plan for delays. Both of our fictional goal setters can work to self-imposed - and in Mrs Brown's case *earlier* - deadlines to give themselves a balanced and structured workload plus proof-reading time plus disaster management time plus I-left-my-work-on-the-bus-and-the-computer-crashed time. Crucially, ask yourself how long it took you to complete a similar project before? How long did it take you to read a novel of a similar length? How long did it take you to write 1,000 words last time you did it? Put (earlier) deadlines in a diary then work backwards creating small steps – what will you achieve one week before or two weeks before the deadline?

Evaluate the process

This stage often gets left out. Divide the year into stages, say three month blocks. At the end of each stage take time to evaluate how well you've used your time. What time-wasting habits could you avoid? Is there anything you have forgotten to schedule? Did you meet your deadlines, self-imposed or otherwise? Why / why not?

Pack a spade

We can apply these specific techniques to virtually any situation where time management is important:

- Prepare. What specific small steps can you take to prepare for your project?
- Action. Take a small step today.
- Create a Master Plan.
- Kick out any time-consuming habits you don't need.
- Advice. Make a list of specific questions and ask someone who's been through it before you.
- Schedule. Block out sessions – a morning, afternoon or evening - in your diary. Set small specific tasks for each.
- Peeks and troughs. Identify the peeks and troughs in your year. Work with them.
- Avoid distractions. Schedule some time for them if they are important.
- Delays. Plan for delays and work out how long it took last time or how long it took to do something similar.
- Evaluate the process.

To remember these tips – and also to emphasize the need for garden time – think of the mnemonic PACK A SPADE.

Practice exercises

Break it down and work out a timeframe

Work out the *smallest* step you would need to take for each of the following. A flowchart, pictures or written instructions are all fine. Use whichever suits you. There is no need to get down to a microscopic level. A small step is *something you could achieve today* – in a couple of minutes, half an hour, or during a morning, afternoon or evening session. Remember the easiest way to work out specifically how long something will take is to think about something similar you've done before. Leave a blank space or add 'research' if there are any gaps in your knowledge. For exercise 5, pick one of your biggest dreams and break it down into small steps.

1. Small steps to apply for a job
2. Small steps to launching a TV Channel

3. Small steps to swim the channel
4. Small steps to travel the world
5. Pick Your Own Dream

Once you've worked through all five, go back and work out a timeframe. Based on what you've written, how long would each goal take? Don't evaluate. If it's 20 years, write 20 years. For the purpose of the exercise, it doesn't matter if you don't think you could do it, work out the steps. We're practising!

Key points
In this chapter we've covered:
1. When time management is important
2. Introducing Mrs Brown and Mr Green
3. Time management basics: time constraints, resources and information, time and space, the big picture, whether it comes with an existing structure
4. Time management specifics: Prepare, Action, Create a Master Plan, Kick out time-consuming habits, Ask for Advice, Schedule, Peeks and troughs, Avoid distractions, Delays, Evaluate the process.
5. Practice exercises: break it down and work out a timeframe.

****

Chapter 11: I Wanted to Change the World But I Could Never Find the Time: Time Management and The Overworked

---

About this chapter

The following exercise regularly came up in school assemblies when I was small: someone has just handed you £1440. Plan how to spend it. The idea behind this exercise is that we have 1440 minutes in everyday. Awareness helps us to spend at least some of them wisely. In this chapter I've applied the £1440 principle to a typical day, week and year, giving you practical exercises to do to look at how you could fit in some small steps towards your goals. I begin by talking about the rhythms and hotspots of life and finish by looking at the peaks and troughs in a year.

Rhythms and hotspots

The rhythms of life

A day, a week, a year, a life-time. Each of these has a rhythm to it. Each has a beginning, middle and end. Each most likely has moments of sadness and joy, mundaneness and wonder. Each has rest times and active times, times for your physical needs, time for family, time for work, time for leisure. Both a year and a life-time have seasons to them.

Think about a typical day

Think about a typical day. Here's an example. This day has a definite a rhythm to it. Imagine it takes you a while to get going in the morning. You make breakfast for the kids and pack them off to school. You still feel sleepy on the train to work. Maybe you're at your desk with a coffee by 9 but you don't really get into your work until 10.30. You have a meeting at 11 – you're on fire, come up with lots of ideas and get noticed by your colleagues. You have a lunch break at 1.30. Until lunch you're confident and breeze through your work easily. After lunch you have a sleepy couple of hours. Then it's wind down time before the commute home. You spend some time with your family, have dinner, watch a bit of TV. You start to feel tired in front of a film and nod off at about midnight.

Rhythms and hotspots: a practical exercise

Introduce awareness into your week. For the next 7 days, record the rhythms of your day and week. Once you know what your rhythms are, time management is much easier to deal with. It's no longer a system that you impose on your life or your particular goal. Rather you can incorporate it, realistically, into your week.

1. Do one of the following:
   - Base your record on the *kind* of activity you are doing – for example health, career, study, family, finances, travel, leisure, social.
   - Base your record on how active or restful you feel on a scale of one to ten, one being asleep and ten being vigorous activity or hard work.
   - Attempt to record your fluctuating emotions – note down how you *feel* about particular tasks. This is tricky because the act of writing it down often changes the emotion!
2. There are certain times during the day when we might feel tense or angry, find it difficult to cope, or which we find particularly stressful. You might also feel particularly hungry or sleepy at certain points. Try to identify these hotspots as you create your rhythm diary.

3. In common with many families apparently – our family has a particular hotspot at the end of the working day when we come in from work and try to cook dinner. Getting out of the house at the beginning of the day is another common hotspot. What are your family hotspots?

Making the hotspots easier

What small steps can you take to make your hotspots easier? Until we realised that we needed some transition time from the work day to the evening – and also to unwind from the commute – it was a source of tension. We planned how to cope with it with simple, small steps. We don't do them all religiously, of course: a change of clothes, a sit down, a glass of water, some time alone, some time catching up *before* starting to cook. One small thing that helped us get out of the house in the morning was a basket. We put keys, bus passes, ID badges and anything that's likely to get lost in the basket. Then we can grab and go before we leave. By the way, it's *not* a good idea to keep this by the door for security reasons.

1440 minutes

1440 minutes: practical exercises

1. What are you doing with yours? Every day you get 1440 minutes to spend. What did you do with yours yesterday? Be as specific as you can. (A difficult task – it's easy to forget how we use our time.)

2. A detailed day-in-the-life. Pick a day when you know you'll have a little bit of leeway to stand back and observe. Not the day of your wedding or driving test or house move or something equally stressful! Nothing too action-packed going on. Record everything you do, with the time it takes you. Carry a notebook. You'll have to do this as you go along: it'll be impossible to remember afterwards in enough detail.

3. Specifics: I'm not implying that any of these things are wrong, far from it, but once you've completed the detailed day-in-the-life activity, look at how much time you spend on specific things. In particular, look at how much time you spend watching TV, preparing and eating meals, sleeping, chatting, staring into space, clearing up. Now look at how much time you spent on:

   - things that *weren't planned*
   - things that were unimportant or unnecessary
   - things that related to the goals you've set

Finding room inside 1440

As I've said before, time management isn't magic. To find time for your goals you've got to become more efficient or stop doing something else. You might also need help organising yourself day-to-day, but that means you'll need to take a step back to do some more observation. Here are the choices. You can:

1. Get up earlier or go to bed later,
2. Delegate or share some of your tasks,
3. Leave work to work hours,
4. Pay someone to do it instead (to clean, to look after the kids, to do the laundry). This obviously creates a financial burden. Even if this is an option for you, it's likely to require sacrifice. Are you prepare to skip your meals out so you can hire a cleaner, for instance?
5. Ask someone to do it for free (could Grandma babysit?) or arrange a skills swap – as long as this still buys you some time,
6. Move from full-time to part-time work or study,
7. Cut down your travel time (share school pick up duties, arrange to work from home, move closer to work)

8. Give something up. If you don't plan for it and just start doing something else, you'll automatically find yourself dropping something. When I wrote my first two novels, my housework and my social life suffered!

9. As a long term strategy, take *longer* to do something. This happened by default with all three of my novels. Because I couldn't work on them fulltime, each took several years to write, which I see as a positive thing – it gave them a chance to mature.

10. Get very good at efficiency techniques. Most time management strategies focus on becoming more efficient. Make it your mission over the next month to collect efficiency strategies – from the internet, from books and magazines, from your friends - and try them out.

Review your detailed day-in-the-life
First ask *why* you want to find more time. Write it down. Then look again at your detailed day-in-the-life. *Aside from becoming more efficient,* where could you find a few minutes out of the 1440 you have everyday to work on your goals or to organise your life? Take some time to prepare, then try it for a few days and record the results. Remember the chapter on reality checking in the previous section! Don't set yourself unrealistic targets. If you already get up at 6, getting up an hour earlier probably isn't an option.

10080: the number of minutes in a week
Giving a week the once over
We've looked at a day close up. Now we're going to give a week the once over. Remember these are guestimates.

- Assuming you sleep for 8 hours a night, you spend 3360 of your 10080 minutes asleep.

- Assuming you spend an hour over breakfast, lunch and dinner, you spend 1260 minutes eating. If you also spend an hour preparing and clearing up each meal, you spend 2520 minutes a week on food. By the way, this is a key area for delegation or sharing tasks or for time-saving gadgets. Could you pre-prepare food for the day all in one go? Would a steamer or a slow cooker help?
- Let's say that between 8 and 11 each evening you wind down, maybe watch some TV or go out to the pub with friends: that's 1260 minutes TV or pub.
- The average commute in the UK, according to the BBC, is 45 minutes. If you spend 90 minutes a day commuting, your total over 5 days is 450.

My weekly count up

OK, it would be excruciating to record the minute detail of your life for a week. You've already had a go at recording your week under 'rhythms and hotspots' so you can use that information for this exercise if it works for you. Also, you can look at the detailed day-in-the-life you recorded and extrapolate.

1. The idea is to take a week and record in your notebook how long you spend on typical tasks. Count your main activity of the day as work whether you're paid for it or not.
   - working,
   - traveling,
   - sleeping,
   - exercising,
   - shopping.

2. Now add some more categories of your own. For example, in one week, how much time do you spend:
   - checking email?

- in meetings?
- shopping?
- cleaning?
- helping your kids with their homework?

3. Check your balance. This is a bit like totting up your bank balance. What did you spend most time on? Anything surprising come up?

A week in detail

Take one part of your life: one that you'd like to change. (This section makes the assumption that you do want to change something in your life!) Keep a detailed record of it. For instance, if you want to be able to sleep better, keep a record of your evening and night-time routine.

If you want to start eating healthily, keep a record of everything you eat and drink. Try not to evaluate, just observe. You can keep going longer than a week if it helps. Before I got pregnant keeping a food diary over three months helped me to identify the extra snacks that were stopping me from losing weight.

Finding room inside 10080

Sometimes we want to incorporate small steps every day. Sometimes once or twice a week works better. It depends what our goal is. Have a look at your weekly expenditure of time.

- Aside from becoming more efficient, is there any time you didn't spend in the best way for you?
- Any time you could use for your goals?
- Again, be realistic. Don't cut out all relaxation, for example. You need to wind down.

525600 minutes and beyond
A year in the life exercise
There are 525600 minutes or 8760 hours in a year. Using the previous exercises take some time to work out (roughly) how much time you spent last year:

- working
- sleeping
- exercising
- going to supermarkets
- concentrating on stuff that's important to you?

The rhythm of the year
A day has a rhythm, as we've discovered, so does a week. All these things, along with the seasons - and the events and traditions associated with them - contribute to the rhythm of the year. The school holidays, Christmas, the long warm days of summer or chilly winter nights all affect how we feel, how we relate to each other and how we relate to the projects we are working on.

Peaks and troughs
We mentioned the idea of peeks and troughs in the last chapter. You've probably noticed that a year has its own cultural peaks and troughs. In this country August and the end of December are trough points. We can speculate about the reasons. It might be because:

- key people are on annual leave so no decisions are made
- large numbers of people *are* kids, or have kids or grandkids, or work with kids! These are the times they're not at school. (In fact parents reading this might be thinking that August and December are actually chock full of activities!)

- we're socialised to think in school holidays from an early age.
- festivals from the past – gathering the harvest and the mid-winter feast - still survive somehow in our collective consciousness.
- we all need downtime and it feels as though the long warm days of the end of summer and the shortest days in the winter are the natural time for it. We've evolved to eat, sleep and reproduce, not to do business 100% of the time!

You can either go with these cultural peaks and troughs, or find the other people who work harder in August and December (presumably to take advantage while the rest are on holiday) and connect with them.

Peaks and troughs exercise
Where are your personal peaks and troughs over the year? When can you take a breath and when does work pile up? For me, work gets stressful when essay marking comes in. This is a 'peak' for me. I have to work very long hours to get it done. It is not a good idea for me to have another deadline at the same time. Knowing when your deadlines are allows you to clear everything else. The best way to do this is to look back on a time you've done something similar. If you've never had a year like the one coming up, re-read the time management specifics in the previous chapter and get as much information as possible in advance.

Your goals over a year: using signposts.
A year is a big enough chunk of time to enable you to work on a sizable project or task, but it is too big to hold in your head all at once. So we use signposts. A signpost is simply a point you want to reach by a particular stage in the year. Signposts are also very handy

for reality-checking. When you create your signposts, think carefully about the peaks and troughs you've identified. If you haven't yet done your Master Plan – whatever method you want to use - do one now with the aim of transposing it onto a calendar or printed year planner. A year planner makes it easier to conceptualise the progress of the project over the year, a calendar (with space to write on it) makes it easier to mingle your small steps with other tasks, appointments and commitments.

1. Add signposts to your calendar or year planner in the following order:
    *   six monthly signposts,
    *   three monthly signposts,
    *   monthly signposts

    Alternatively, add a signpost every twelve to fifteen weeks, with a review every six to twelve weeks. If you find the process difficult, it may be easier to work backwards from the point at which you wish to successfully finish the project or achieve your goal, like you did with the one of the flowcharts at the beginning of this book.

2. Once you've put in your signposts, you're free to block out morning, afternoon or evening sessions so you can work on your project. Personally I add these scheduled sessions to the family calendar *and* my diary but you may not need to. At this stage you can check to see whether you've been overly ambitious: Will you finish making the film you've always dreamed about by the end of the year if you only have one session a week to work on it?

3. Now decide which small steps you'll do on a weekly (or even a daily) basis. Put in up to six week's worth. Remember to add time to review your plan.

This technique also works for longer projects of 3, 5, 10 and 20 years. For example: *In 5 years time I will travel around the world* or *In 10 years time I will have paid off my mortgage.* Put in yearly signposts, then six monthly, then three and one monthly signposts, or add a signpost every twelve to fifteen weeks. After that don't forget the crucial stage: block out sessions and create weekly small steps, with review time built in.

Finding room inside 525600
Take into account the rhythm of your year and examine your calendar or year planner.

- Is there a point when you could take some time off to work on a particular project in one solid chunk?
- Is there a point when you could plan some special time with people who are important to you?
- Could you volunteer once a month?
- Go to the library once a fortnight?
- If you work on your project every weekend for a year, what will you have to sacrifice?
- Build in some time off, too.

Key points
In this chapter, we've covered:
1. Rhythms and hotspots
2. 1440 minutes
3. Finding room inside 1440
4. Giving a week the once over
5. My weekly count up
6. Finding room inside 10080
7. A year in the life exercise
8. The rhythm of the year and peaks and troughs
9. Your goals over a year: using signposts
10. Finding room inside 525600

Chapter 12: Set It Up, Break It Down, Make It Easy

About this chapter

In this chapter we learn the crucial aspects of small steps time management: set it up, break it down, make it easy. The examples given in this chapter use pretty major goals like building a house, writing a novel and making £25000. But the *set it up, break it down, make it easy* strategy applies equally to everyday tasks and time management at work too, and any of the goals you set in the first section of the book. By the way, have a quick look at the resources section for a fascinating article on the psychology behind 'making it easy'.

Set it up

Set up what?

Some of your small steps will be about setting up your work space and maintaining it, and organising your life. Using the following guidelines, you'll set up:

- Your spaces
- Your lifestyle and your support network
- Your routine
- Your chores and admin
- Your equipment

Your spaces

For everything you want to achieve, and for all of your day-to-day tasks, make sure the space is set up as well as it can be. Think you don't need a space set up? Work with the main space where your goal, project or task will take place. For instance, if you aim to eat healthily 80% of the time for a year, your space is your *main cooking area* and anywhere you store shopping and cooking paraphernalia. *Even if* you still think you don't need a space set up to achieve your goal, have a space to think.

Think CHECK
Your priorities for setting up your spaces are calmness, happiness, ergonomics, comfort, and - another mnemonic - KISS (keep it simple stupid).

Calmness. Can you instil a sense of calm and safety in the space, rather than disorder and mayhem? Even if disorder and mayhem are important as part of your final project – you might be organising a carnival or a puppet show for two year olds! – there are at least some aspects, particularly in the planning stages, that will need some serenity.

- Happiness. I don't mean pleasure or contentedness. Obviously we can't feel pleasure all the time, although arguably having a notebook or a photograph on your desk that gives you pleasure will help. Make sure there isn't anything about your space that, in the back of your mind, reminds you of something annoying or distressing. An empty notebook might make you feel frustrated that you haven't filled it, a photo might make you sad. As a general principle, keep your own and other people's happiness in mind when organising your space. If your office is the place you retreat to after an argument it won't feel happy. Sharing your new garage workshop so both you and your partner can work on projects equally is likely to make you both happier.
- Ergonomics. How user-friendly is the space you've set up and the equipment you've got? How easy is it to get at? Consider the small things: any tools you need, paper,

envelopes, pens, notebooks, stamps and bigger systems such as filing. Is anything in the way? This applies to setting up the kitchen if you want to eat more healthily, too. Try to make it as easy as possible to make healthy food. Get a steamer and set it up ready to use, for instance.

- Comfort. If you bang your head every time you go into your space or your chair gives you a bad back or it's very cold, it will affect your relationship with your project. Eventually the project itself will start to annoy you because you'll associate it with a sore head, a bad back and feeling cold. As a general principle, it's *not* a good idea to suffer for your project. Psychologically speaking, the more uncomfortable it makes you, the less likely you are to continue with it.

- KISS. This is good advice in most areas of our lives. When it comes to organising our spaces, often experts will advise us to use particular spaces for one thing. For instance, keep the bedroom for sleeping. I've heard of a novelist who writes in two genres so she has two writing spaces, one for crime, one for romance. Sometimes it isn't possible or even preferable to do this. Instead we can try to keep some spaces simple, even if others are cluttered. Or we can turn one room into two different spaces. Using a very good filing system, a bedroom could be an office in the morning but a bedroom in the afternoon and evening, if there's nowhere else to work. Keep the space as simple as possible.

Your lifestyle.

We also need to set up our lifestyle to make time management easier. Take a look at your typical week from the exercise you did in the last chapter. How structured or unstructured is it? How structured would you like it to be? You can use CHECK to set it up:

- Calmness. Make sure you build in some moments of calm – or at least moments of pause - into each day and each week.

- Happiness. Does your lifestyle make you happy? Sure, there will be challenges, but is it satisfying, does it allow you to stop and think from time to time, and do you have time for the people and projects that are important to you? What can you do about anything in your life that's far too stress-inducing or unsatisfying?

- Ergonomics. How user-friendly is your lifestyle? Look at your typical day and week again. Could you make any of your regular tasks easier to do? Could your journey to work, your social life, your exercise routine, cleaning tasks, or shopping habits get any more user-friendly? For example – and of course these won't work for everyone - take the train to work so you can read as you go, shop online to avoid overspending, agree to a babysitting rota with friends, or go jogging so you can skip the gym fees.

- Comfort. I'm not talking about overindulgence in food, drink, drugs or consumer goods here. I'm talking about kindness. Are you being kind to yourself? (And it's a good idea to be kind to yourself, in case you're wondering!) It's well known advice: do something nice for yourself everyday. Is your life all get up and go or is there some cushion time? Furthermore, *do you take care of your basic needs?* Yes, challenges make us stronger, but there's no virtue in suffering for no reason, especially as it makes you less able to help other people.

- KISS. Simplify your life and your living spaces as much as you can. Take a look at your typical day and your typical week. Is anything more complex than it needs to be?

Set up your support network

It's easy to forget that we can be *proactive* when it comes support networks. It's also easy to feel pretty desperate about a lack of support network. Reread the section on support in the previous section and go out and find some like-minded people. A support network is about quiet chats or hanging out as well as having a good laugh or joining an organised group.

- Could you simplify your week to allow more time to simply hang out with friends?

Set up your routine.

If it helps, make sure you have a record of everything you need to get done on a day-to-day basis and the *specifics* of any small steps that you would also like to achieve each day or week. You probably already have a list of these small steps elsewhere in your notebook. If you've been working through this book you should have a pretty good idea of what to include by now. Try the list exercise below if you need to work out how to fit your goals into your daily and weekly routines.

The list exercise

1. Create a list that includes the specifics of anything you want to do regularly each day. The idea is to create a *daily routine* which becomes habit forming.
2. Create a weekly routine. Use sessions – morning, afternoon or evening – and write in anything you want to do regularly each week. Schedule anything that can't be moved, like meetings or classes or start / finish times. From looking at

these routines it should be clear whether you're trying to do too much. Adjust as necessary.

3. You might want to do two lists, one for work and one for home to enable you to treat work projects separately.

Your chores and admin

Set up your daily and weekly chores so that they become part of the routine and so that they are as user-friendly as possible. Everyone has admin to do, financial or otherwise. Build this into your weekly routine and it won't pile up.

Your equipment

For any goals you want to achieve, for daily and weekly routine tasks and for chores and administration, you need equipment, including stationery and storage space. Take some time to review what you need. Make sure you set it up in the most user-friendly way possible. Make it accessible and secure. This process doesn't have to be expensive. If you do need special equipment you don't have, try freecycle or ebay for example. Start off as simple as you can. In fact, see this as a simplification process rather than a complication process. What's the most simple and appropriate way to equip yourself?

Don't let lack of equipment stop you from starting out. The beginning of any project – the ground work, training or research – can often be achieved for free or through volunteering your time. Keep a list of anything you need to buy as part of your research rather than i) splurging all your savings immediately or ii) writing off the project as too expensive.

Remember that raising the money to achieve your goals can also be broken down into small steps.

Break it down
Breaking it down to manage your time

Now you'll apply what you've already learnt about breaking down your projects, tasks and goals into small steps. You'll also read two examples of how this technique works in practice. Once you've broken down the task, however complicated, into small chunks, you should be able to work out how long it is likely to take and to plan accordingly.

Take any big task that doesn't fit easily into your routine and write it out in your notebook if you haven't already done so. Naming it like this is a big start. Include notes on your timeframe for the task. What's the deadline? Or how long do you think it will take? How long did it take you last time you did something similar?

The component parts

What are the component parts of this task? Is anyone else involved? Be as concrete and specific as you can. For example, imagine a fictional person called Martin. His goal, simply stated, is *I want to build my own house*. It initially breaks down into research, design, finance, and possibly training. Once the project is underway, he might have new headings such as administration, project management, budget, infrastructure, plumbing and wiring etc etc. Naming the parts like this allows Martin to allocate time to each one and to work out how long each will take.

Take steps backwards

You need a year planner or a diary for this exercise.

1. Look at the big task you've identified again. Decide on the results you want. Where do you want to be? What do you want to achieve? Visualise it.
2. Start with the end result and work backwards. Each small step is something you could achieve on one

day. Use your diary or year planner to work out *when* you're likely to achieve what you want and *how long* you will need to spend on small steps each week. Have you got small enough? Have you gone far enough back?

3. If you find any blocks along the way or anything you need to research or ask advice about, make a list.

4. Take any apparent block. What would it mean to overcome this block? What would it look like? Again take small steps backwards from the results you want. Write them down.

Do you need any new knowledge or advice?

Now Martin has broken down the task, he should be able to identify areas to research, people to consult, or knowledge and advice he doesn't have. For example, *I want to build my own house* leads to research tasks such as: talk to someone who's done it, find out how to buy a plot of land, find out about plumbing classes in his area.

Something you can do today

Remember that your aim is to break the task down until you get to something you can do today, noting any barriers along the way, including emotional barriers. For example, today Martin could spend one session finding internet forums for environmentally friendly DIY home-builders.

Review your timeframe

Now you've broken down the task into small chunks, use a year planner or diary and review how long you think it will take. Look at the time you will need to dedicate to the task – over days, weeks, months or years – to do it justice. What's the monthly, weekly and daily commitment? Can you fit it into your routine?

Break it down example: raising money.

I need to raise £25,000.

This might well be the first, separate, goal when Martin breaks down *build my own house*. Imagine, for a moment, that time is no barrier at all. It frees you up to think creatively. You'll notice that its *time* that's the issue here, not your ability to raise the money.

Raising £25,000 is the same as raising £2500 10 times. Raising £2500 is the same as raising £250 10 times. Raising £250 is the same as raising £25 10 times. (And of course, if you happen to be raising money for a good cause, asking everyone you know to ask everyone *they* know to give £2.50 is a good start!)

What could you do today?

The prospect of saving up a large amount can be daunting, but you've got to start somewhere and I bet you could do one of these:

1. Find something in your house worth £25 that you don't use to auction online.
2. Look at your bank account and make a saving of £25 by cancelling a subscription or membership you don't use.
3. Save £25 on your shopping by making a shopping list, downgrading brands, planning to use leftovers or making better use of your freezer.
4. Start a savings account and set up a standing order for £25 a month or make your savings work harder by moving to a better rate.
5. Move your credit card debt to a 0% deal and save more than £25 on interest payments.
6. Move your household bills to different providers to save money – probably more than £25 a time.
7. Save at least £25 by buying items you use a lot in bulk when they are on special offer. For instance, a

pack of cards is cheaper than buying birthday cards year round.

8. Shop early for Christmas to avoid being taken in by attractive advertising.
9. Save £5 a day for a week by taking packed lunch to work.
10. Do you have a skill you can sell or could you learn one? I bet you could make at least £25 from one of **ideas listed on the website.**

Too much effort?

It might seem like an uphill struggle to get to £25000 in £25 increments, but don't forget two things:

- You've decided that your goal is something you really want – if you've worked through this book then you'll have set a goal you're interested in.
- Look back at the W. H. Murray quotation about commitment in chapter five. Once you commit, the magic starts to happen. Or rather, being proactive about money will make it work for you! 'Magic' might just mean making confirmation bias work for you.

But is it worth it?

Of course, many of the skills on the list on the website are fun to practise even if you don't make money from them! There's much to be gained from volunteering these skills or skills exchange. And not everything we do can possibly have a numerical value attached – activities like spending time with our families, relaxation and doing the best we can to be healthy are all priceless. Having said all that, if your aim is to make some money towards your target of £25000, and you have a plan to earn extra - work out if it's worth it first.

- How much do you cost in your day job?
- How much can you earn per hour, PAYE or freelance?
- How much tax would you pay on the extra you earn?
- How much could earn in the private sector doing what you do?

It may not be worth doing something extra that sees a considerably lower return for the hours put in. Even on the minimum wage, ten minutes work is worth a pound, at the time of writing. You've also got to consider how much *time* you will allocate to each new money making project, including research and preparation time.

It may be worth employing someone to do some tasks, such as cleaning. How much are you 'paying yourself' to do the work? These tasks may take up time when you could be earning money through higher paid work.

There might be something more radical (and risky) you could do to raise money – of course with the advice and support of an expert – such as investing in property or stocks and shares or changing your job. These kinds of decisions can't be taken lightly. See a financial advisor if you need help.

Break it down example: writing a novel.
I want to write 100,000 words
Imagine you plan to write a novel of around 100, 000 words. Once more, imagine for a moment that time is no barrier at all, because it allows you to think creatively. Assuming that you can string a sentence together, you'll soon discover that the issue here is not whether you are capable of writing 100,000 words, it's a matter of how much *time* you give to the project. You don't write that much

in one go. You write however many words you usually write in one session, whether that's 250, 500, 1000 or 5000. You'll find that 100,000 words means:

- 100 sessions spent writing 1000 words
- 200 sessions spent writing 500 words.
- 1000 sessions spent writing 100 words.
- Or think of it this way: if you write 250 words a day, you'll be close to your target by the end of the year.

How to divide your time
A novel needs at least four more things:

- Planning time
- Research time
- Editing time
- Marketing time

Small steps to writing a novel
I don't have space to go into these things in detail here, but note that *writing* time is separate from planning, research, editing and marketing time. Again each is simply a matter of thinking up small steps, allocating *time* and turning up:

- Once you have given yourself the time and space to write, you can actually let go of the outcome and simply turn up.
- Of course, if you are working to a pre-existing deadline, you'll need to do the opposite. Divide up the time you have available and set up word length targets along the way.
- Make sure the time you give is appropriate. Remember that time management isn't a magic wand. To do it, you'll have to *not do* something else or become more efficient.

- To use this strategy, *you need to know how long it takes you to write 1000 words.* I suggest taking a short course or doing some toe-dipping practice sessions before making the final commitment.

- Practice is much more important than talent. Practice is concrete and specific – you can schedule it, you can turn up. Talent is rather vague and hard to define. Also, it doesn't matter how talented you are, unless you practice no-one will ever know. For more on this see Matthew Syed's book *Bounce*, which I reviewed briefly in chapter seven.

- You'll notice that 'novel writing' isn't included in the list of possible money-making skills in the first example of breaking it down. That's because you almost certainly won't recoup a reasonable amount of money, given the time put in.

Using subheadings to break down tasks

Mind the gap

Many hands make light. Great minds think. Too many cooks spoil. Our brains don't like gaps and try very hard to fill them in – as yours probably just demonstrated with the last three unfinished sentences. You can put this capacity to fill gaps to your advantage using the subheading technique. By the way, it's easier after you've researched, read up on or talked to someone about whatever you're doing a little bit first, because you'll have slightly more contextual knowledge that way. Here's how you do it:

1. First divide the task into its component parts. If you don't know for sure, it's ok to guess at this point. Write them down in your notebook.

2. Take a piece of paper and write out the task at the top. Use the space on the page to provide gaps for your brain to fill in. Write the numbers 1 to 5 down

the page. Under each one of these write the letters a, b, c.

3. Now think of five main subheadings relating to the task. Space them out down the page next to the numbers 1 to 5. Under each one – next to the letters a, b, c - write three mini-subheadings. There's something about leaving gaps (or telling your brain it needs to think up a certain number of things) that gets you filling them in.

4. Use your research or any expert advice you've received at this stage. If you know you'll have to write a business plan or seek financial advice, then these can easily transpose into subheadings or mini-subheadings.

5. Use colour to mark any gaps in your knowledge or any research points. Sometimes a task seems impossible simply because of these gaps. Create a list of research tasks instead. For example: "I can't do it. I know nothing about it" – very vague, and very negative - becomes:

    - On Monday morning, spend an hour looking into financial advisors in this area.
    - On Saturday afternoon, go to a Prince's Trust seminar on running your own business.

Adaptations
- Use a giant piece of paper – as large as you can – and add images and colour.
- Use a computer to create your subheadings. You don't have to worry so much about setting up your page.
- Use more subheadings 1 to 10 for instance and more mini-subheadings a – e for instance.

- You can also successfully adapt these approaches and apply them to mind mapping. Have a look at Tony Buzans work, which I reviewed briefly in chapter seven.

Essay writing example

The subheading technique works well for students who need to write an essay. Here's how:

1. First divide the essay question into component parts. Write them down in your notebook. Go word-by-word through the question if you have to. For example, *How did the cholera epidemic in New York City in 1832 affect population growth?* Breaks down into 'cholera epidemic', 'New York City in 1832' and 'population growth'.

2. Check for hidden parts. Remember I said that it's easier to use the subheading technique after you've researched, read up on or talked to someone about whatever you're doing a little bit first? There are some hidden parts to this question – most importantly water and sanitation – that you'd only know about if you had a bit of knowledge about cholera outbreaks.

3. You need context. You're also going to need some contextual information about New York City and population growth before and after 1832. This is the case with most essays and is where your studying comes in!

4. Take a large piece of paper and write out the essay question at the top. Use the space on the page to provide gaps for your brain to fill in. Write the numbers one to five down the page, under each one of these write the letters a to c.

5. You can change the number of subheadings and mini-subheadings to suit the essay length. Add more gaps if the essay is going to be a long one, say 1 to 10 and a – e. Include fewer gaps if the essay is fairly short, say 1 – 3 and a, b.

6. Now think of some main subheadings that relate back to the original essay question. Space them out down the page next to the numbers one to five. Phrase them as questions if possible. Under each subheading write some mini-subheadings that relate to that section of the essay. These are going to divide into paragraphs. How many depends on the essay length.

7. Use course guidance at this stage. If the tutor has told you to include three things covered in seminars, or if you have to include books by three different authors, then these can easily transpose into subheadings or mini-subheadings.

8. Based on the word limit, how many words will you write on each mini-subheading? For example, a 2000 word essay could divide into 5 sections of 400 words, each with a subheading. Those 400 word sections could divide into 2 paragraphs of 200 words, each with a mini-subheading.

9. Check for connections and links. Check for connections between sections that you can make reference to: draw arrows in a different colour. How will you link each paragraph to the previous one?

10. Use colour to mark any gaps in your knowledge or any research points. Sometimes a written piece of work seems impossible simply because of these gaps. Turn them into a list of tasks. For example: "This

essay is impossible. I know nothing about it" – very vague, and very negative - becomes:

- On Monday morning, go to the library and look up the rate of population growth New York City between 1800 and 1832.
- Spend evenings next week reading the relevant parts of Massimo Bacci's book *A Concise History of World Population* and *The Cholera Years* by Charles E. Rosenberg.

Any written piece of work

You can use the same subheading technique to plan any written piece of work, including long projects. You can use it for websites, in house magazines, newsletters or brochures, for example. This book was planned using this subheading technique. By the way, Randy Ingermanson applies a version of 'subheadings' to the novel writing process using the Snowflake Method. First published online, there's now more about the Snowflake Method in *Writing Fiction For Dummies*.

I want to build my own house

In fact, you can use the subheading technique to plan any project at all *because writing it down is a little like thinking on the page.* Imagine our fictional self-builder, Martin, uses the subheading technique:

1. He creates numbered gaps on a sheet of paper and comes up with five subheadings.
2. Under each one he creates mini –subheadings on specific aspects of the project.
3. Under each mini –subheading he writes bullet points, or specific tasks, or describes an aspect of the project as it currently stands.

4. He marks up in colour any knowledge gaps or research points. This will help him to separate out anything that currently feels impossible from aspects of the project that he could achieve this year, this month, this week, or today.

Knowledge gaps

As with the essay, sometimes a project seems impossible simply because of knowledge gaps. Using the same principles, you can turn them into a list of tasks. So the vague and negative: "I'll never build my own house, I can't even change a plug" becomes:

- On Saturday afternoon, investigate beginners' DIY courses.
- Have a pizza night on Thursday and look into self-build mortgages.
- On the way home from picking the kids up from school on Wednesday, see if the library has any books on self-build houses.

Make it easy

All systems go

In this chapter, we've talked already about how comfort and ease make it *more likely* that you'll get a task done. Using the CHECK system, you should have already set up your projects, tasks and goals to make them calm, happy, ergonomic, comfy and simple. Your projects will still be a challenge but this short final part to the chapter allows you to check that your systems really are as easy to use as possible. Here are some practical exercises and ideas to help you to make it easy.

1. *What do you see? What do you use?*
   Sit or stand in your work space. What can you see? Anything annoying, stress-inducing, upsetting? Get rid of it. Anything you never use? Get rid of it. Anything that needs

filing? Sort it out. Could you make it simpler? Calmer? Happier? What do you use in this space? Is it easy to reach? Easy to use? Does it annoy me? Why? Is everything easy to use and easy to find?

2. *What bugs you?*

    Keep a bugs diary. We've did a shorter version of this exercise earlier in chapter eight when we looked at motivation and you wrote a list of small niggles that annoy you, interrupt you, frustrate you or prevent you from doing what you want to do. Do it again but this time carry your notebook with you all day and note *anything at all* that bugs you, including trains of thought, if you can manage to catch hold of them, news items, bad customer service or the way you relate to people and they to you. Bugs can be more general, abstract and random than the niggles you wrote about before.

3. *What's difficult?*

    Focus on one day and record anything you find particularly difficult or complicated.

4. *De-cluttering*

    Make it easy by getting rid of the junk. Spend some time recycling, swapping, and using online buying and selling sites.

5. *Use small tools*

    Stick up whiteboards, put pens where they are easy to get to, keep ongoing shopping lists on the wall, put clocks and calendars where you can see them, make sure your keys are easy to find. More on this later.

Case study: Applying set it up, break it down, make it easy.

I want to build my own house. Here our fictional self-builder, Martin, sets his spare room up, breaks it down and makes it easy:

1. Setting it up. Martin is going to spend Saturday afternoons working on his project. Initially he needs some office space. He sets it up so he can get to his files easily. He picks up some magazine holders on freecycle and uses a box for library books so he doesn't forget to return them. With his partner he creates a collage of all the things they'd like in their dream house: it's going to be environmentally friendly, with a room for everyone in the family, a utility room and a play room. There will be a treehouse in the garden. Martin keeps this on his desk along with a picture drawn by his children. He sticks up a whiteboard so his to do list is visible all the time.

2. Breaking it down. We already know that Martin's goal initially breaks down into research, design, finance, and training. He breaks it down further and decides to spend this year doing a plumbing and electrical course at the local college in the evenings. His partner does some weekend workshops on interior design. In the meantime, they try to get their finances in order by keeping on top of them once a week, seeing a financial advisor, paying down their debts and setting up a savings account. His partner usually makes small Christmas presents for family. This year they make extra and sell them. Martin confines his research to borrowing books from the library on the subject. Notice the couple's extra financial commitment so far comes down to paying for the classes and materials for the presents. Eventually – using small steps - the present making turns into a small business.

3. Make it easy. Here are some of the things Martin does to make it as easy as possible. Again, notice how there is minimal financial commitment here – these are all small steps:

- He calls in at the library on the way back from picking his kids up from school.
- He picks an evening class as close as possible to where he lives.
- He sells old clothes on ebay, making it part of his routine to check in every morning.
- He sets up a standing order to his savings account.
- He clears all the clutter within five feet of his desk, piles it up and sorts through it over a weekend. Much of it goes into the recycling or on recycling website.

Key points

In this chapter we've covered:

1. Set up your spaces, your lifestyle, your support network, your routine, your chores and admin, your equipment. Think CHECK.
2. Break it down: the component parts, taking steps backwards, new knowledge or advice. Something you can do today, reviewing your timeframe.
3. Break it down examples: raising money and writing a novel.
4. Using subheadings to break down tasks. Writing an essay and building your own house.
5. Practical exercises and ideas to help you to make it easy.
6. Case study: Applying set it up, break it down, make it easy.

****

Chapter 13: Make It Count, Keep It Balanced, Think Whole Picture

About this chapter

We cover three more crucial parts of small steps time management in this chapter: make it count, keep it balanced, and think whole picture. Under 'make it count' you'll learn four ways to make sure you're spending your time in the best possible way: doing whatever you're doing and being present, concentrating on the important stuff, staying task-focused, and flexibility. In the second section, 'keep it balanced', you'll be introduced to balanced time management and the importance of incorporating THESE and THEM into your schedule. We'll do more on balanced time management in the next chapter. Finally you'll look at convergent and divergent thinking – first touched on in chapter two - and try some divergent thinking exercises.

Make it count

Doing whatever you're doing

Making it count means focusing on the present moment. Buddhist philosophers talk about being present in each moment, exhibiting mindfulness, rather than drifting through life unaware of our surroundings or the reasons we're doing what we're doing. This means, rather than longing to achieve your goals so much that the present – perhaps rather mundane - task becomes an annoyance, do whatever you're doing fully, wholeheartedly. Being aware makes us *make the tasks count* whether we see them as ordinary or extraordinary. Some of the following small steps will be familiar but they are easy to forget. Write them up somewhere you can see them if you need to. Each of the following small steps will keep you more aware of how you spend your time:

- Take a deep breath before each new task.
- Take regular breaks.
- Appreciate at least one ordinary task a day, as fully as you can. Making the tea for instance.
- Use the Pomodoro Technique. (See the resources section.) Giving yourself limited time to do a task – and focusing on it fully - tends to make you super-aware.

How do you define 'important'?

Making it count also means doing the important stuff. Several self-help gurus suggest that tasks can be categorised as important or non-important, urgent or non-urgent. We tend to do urgent non-important things first whereas, so the advice goes, it's better to prioritize *non-urgent important tasks* instead. Easier said than done in an age of information overload.

One serious problem with this advice is how 'important' is defined. I've used the word 'important' over a hundred times in this book and have left you to decide what it means! Part of achieving balanced time management means working out what important means and doing it. But so that we can take this particular piece of advice seriously, it's worth looking at some slightly different meanings of the term:

1. The self-help gurus who urge us to do the important stuff first seem to mean that important = *chimes with your values*. In order to implement this advice you need to know what your values are.

2. Important could also mean *the thing that most needs your attention right now.*

3. Important might also mean *a task that will make a difference to your life and help you achieve your goals.*

4. Important is likely to mean different things at work and at home. If you need to work to survive, to a certain extent *whatever is important at work* has to be given priority while you're doing it.

It follows that if you spend most of your time doing things that don't chime with your values you'll be unhappy, and that if you do a job – paid or unpaid - involving your personal values and the goals you've set, you'll be more satisfied with it.

We need to allocate appropriate amounts of time to each important thing in our lives. Preparation is key to this idea. That said, adopting *do the important stuff first* as a mantra does force you to become more aware of how you use your time.

Non-urgent but important
For this next practical exercise, assume that important = *will make a difference to my life and help me achieve my goals.*

- Start by identifying at least four non-urgent but important tasks. Break them down into small steps
- Allocate time to carry out each small step. I suggest one per week at first.
- Go through your diary and add them in advance.
- After a month review what you've done so far and set yourself some more non-urgent but important tasks. Break them down as before.
- Eventually aim to do at least one non-urgent but important small step per day, preferably at the start of the day.
- Use your routine to limit the time you spend on urgent non-important tasks. Email, for example, can

easily get you embroiled in tasks that are urgent but non-important.

What about non-important non-urgent stuff?
Have a cardboard folder for interesting articles, organised by topic if necessary, and for any materials (including your own ideas) that you'd like to keep but don't know what to do with. Also use this file for any projects you'd like to complete that – at the moment – are non-important non-urgent. That way you (and your desk) won't get bogged down with non-important non-urgent stuff, but you'll be able to find whatever it is if it suddenly makes you curious. Create a digital version of this folder to store ideas and articles you've found online.

For example, I like to collect recipes. You could argue that my collection is important just because I like doing it. Fair enough. On the other hand, you could argue that this task isn't important. I wouldn't save my recipe collection if my house was on fire. I'm not a chef and I'm not planning to become one. It's certainly not urgent. Rather than abandoning my recipe collection, or agonising over how important it is and descending into nihilistic-angst, I've just made it easy to tear out and store the recipes, so it takes a matter of seconds. I also have a recipe folder on my computer desktop.

What you're doing IS important
Making it count also means the opposite. Look at it this way: what you're doing IS important. Sometimes we can mentally downgrade very important tasks and feel that if we're not directly earning money or we're not out achieving a whole range of goals, then we must be failing. This is especially true if we tend to apply a business model to everything we do. Depending on your situation, looking after your baby is important, picking up your kids from school is

important, spending time with your parents is important. Sometimes (again depending on your situation) it's better to concentrate on doing what we're doing, without trying to multi-task. This isn't a contradiction of all I've said about goal-setting: instead, it's about time. There's time to do what you're doing now. Set aside time to do the rest, too, if you want to.

Stay task-focused

Making it count is about staying task-focused. You've planned to use your time in a particular way – now do it. As much as possible, forget about personalities, blame, guilt and not feeling like it. (If you can't, keep a notebook and jot it all down before you start.) Now, if you've set yourself a task and allocated a session to complete it, *keep coming back to the task*. Every time you wander off (either literally or metaphorically) come back, until your session is over:

- What is it, specifically, that you've set aside time to do? Each time you start doing something else – checking your email, logging on to social networking sites, washing up – come back to the specifics of it.
- Use the space you've set up to structure your task. Sit at your desk or get down on the yoga mat or hang out in your workshop for the full session. Give yourself a bit of time to bookend your session, to warm up or warm down, again using the space.

Flexibility

Making it count is also about flexibility. Sometimes flexibility is seen as one of those soft skills that everyone says they're good at but are ultimately very hard to define. We're probably all set in our ways to a certain extent, and in certain situations, and flexible in others. Here are some ways to develop your flexibility:

- Offer to cover for your partner, a friend or colleague and ask them to return the favour.

- Snatch little bits of time to work on a task (or to think about it) when you're waiting for something or queuing.
- Carry your notebook, or digital equivalent, everywhere.
- Do something different once a week: go a different route, use a new café, walk instead of riding the bus, wear your hair up, sleep on the other side of the bed, eat waffles for breakfast instead of fruit, use a different brand, buy tea instead of coffee.
- Schedule sessions in your diary and turn up for them but incorporate flexibility by reviewing your plan every six to twelve weeks.

Some things are worth being stubborn about! Remember that you're trying to make changes to your daily, weekly and sometimes monthly routines, to incorporate your goals, so stick at it. If you always end up doing something else instead of the activity you planned, schedule sessions at a different time rather than berating yourself.

Keep it balanced
Your year pie chart
First of all let's look at how you spent your year. Think about the last 12 months when you do this exercise:

1. Either use the headings 'health, career, study, family, finances, travel, leisure, social' or the life parts you came up with in the first part of the book. How much time do you think you spent on each of these over the last twelve months? Work it out by averaging what you do over a typical week and calculating an actual percentage of your time; otherwise, you have my permission to guess! Give each

life part a chunk of the pie. Small chunk = not much time. Large chunk = lots of time.

2. Look over your year pie chart. Which life part (aside from sleeping) got the biggest slice of the pie? Are you spending time on each area that is important to you?

What is balanced time management?

There's no way that we can achieve all our goals at once, or involve ourselves in every hobby and interest from animation to flower arranging to orienteering to sports coaching to zoology. Therefore we need balanced time management. Balance *doesn't* mean trying to cram activities from lots of different categories, like pub quiz questions: art, sport, nature, science etcetera. To make the ideas behind balanced time management easy to remember, think THESE and THEM! All will be revealed below.

THESE

As we've discussed before, many time management strategies focus on enabling us to use time more efficiently, so that we can perform individual tasks more quickly or competently. Ok, but our health and general wellbeing is so important that it would be ridiculous to leave it of the mix. I've broken down health and wellbeing into Taking care of yourself, Healthy Eating, Sleeping well and Exercise. Remember the acronym THESE:

- Taking care of yourself includes relaxation, getting checked out by the doctor if you need to, doing something about stress, being kind to yourself. It also includes taking care of your social and spiritual wellbeing and looking after your relationships.
- Healthy eating will mean different things to different people but roughly translates to following the 80 / 20 rule, that is, try to be healthy 80% of the time; getting the rainbow of

fruit and veg you need; knowing a bit about food, what you need and what it does to your body.

- Sleeping well, as a concept, is pretty self-explanatory though it's sometimes hard to achieve. Do some research so you know how to get a good night's sleep; create a bedtime routine and a relaxing sleep environment; don't repeatedly put work before sleep.

- Exercise. Be active. Walk, garden, swim. It doesn't have to be complicated or expensive.

Healthy eating

Let's take food as an example, and apply the small steps method. When it comes to food and health everyone is different and you should, of course, see a health professional if you need advice. We learnt in the opening chapter of this book that food is on the bottom rung of Maslow's *Hierarchy of Needs* meaning that we have to sort it out *first* before trying to achieve anything else.

1. What small steps could you take so that you could eat a healthy breakfast 80% of the time? For example:
   a. Make it the night before or in advance
   b. Buy or make some healthy grab-and-go snacks every week.
   c. Put a breakfast menu on the wall
   d. Get up a bit earlier so you can take your time
   e. Keep a food diary for a week. When you review it, think particularly about how to build in more healthy breakfasts.

2. What small steps would you need to take so that you keep your blood sugar level balanced? For example:
   a. Do some research into G.I. foods or foods and moods at your local library or on the internet.

    b.   Carry some healthy snacks with you and take time to eat them.

    c.   Where you can switch from white to brown foods, such as pasta, rice and bread.

    d.   Improve how you eat at work, especially the snacks you have in meetings and on coffee breaks when your mind is on something else.

    e.   Add to your food diary. Identify the times you're most likely to get hungry and reach for a sugary snack.

3.   What small steps would you need to take so that you eat enough fruit and veg each week? For example:

    a.   Change your attitude. Decide what fruit and veg you actually like so it doesn't feel like a punishment!

    b.   Keep a fruit bowl in the middle of the table and on your desk at work.

    c.   Use a liquidiser to add fruit and veg to sauces and to make your own smoothies.

    d.   Look into fruit and veg deliveries.

    e.   Add to your food diary. Tally up your fruit and veg count at the end of each day.

THESE and other people

You may also be involved in helping others to keep THESE in mind, especially if you're a boss or you have a partner or a best friend or a family to look after. For example:

- Taking care of yourself. *"Yes, I'll stay at work until 8pm tonight to finish a project but I'll come home early on Friday and give my partner a night off."*

- Sleeping well. *"No, I won't buy a new flat screen TV because we really need a more comfortable mattress."*

Making time for THESE

When you're thinking about time management, when you're breaking down tasks, creating routines and allocating sessions, make time every week for THESE and you're likely to feel better about the rest of your tasks and will probably achieve them more quickly.

THEM

No, I'm not talking creatures from outer space. Pairing THEM with THESE is a quick way to remember that spending time with our friends and family is a huge part of keeping our lives balanced. Yes, 'us' would be a more accurate way to describe this idea but THEM and THESE gives you a handy mnemonic! When you're creating weekly and monthly routines, allow time to do things with the people who are important to you. In return, when you give people time like this, they (usually!) respect the sessions you've scheduled to work on your goals. Obviously allowing time for others encourages collaboration and communication too. Balanced time management means keeping THESE and THEM in mind when thinking about how you spend your time. Take some small steps today, for instance:

- Make time to *plan* being with people rather than sitting back and letting it happen. Be proactive about it.
- Do simple and low-cost things like walks in the park or coffee and chat.
- Use a calendar to schedule meetings and activities and keep it in view.
- Use social networking or email to stay in touch regularly.
- Arrange to do a regular activity together. Take the kids swimming once a week, for instance.
- Aaron Craze, chef and TV presenter, appeared on Blue Peter to talk about his family's tombola. All three members of his family write down four things they want to do – giving

them one for each month of the year. They pick one from a hat once a month and go and do it!

All about THEM

Here's a rough guide to planning your time with family and friends:

- Family. You can define family in whatever way you like, but get some family time into your schedule once a day and once a week. As a rule of thumb if you regularly have no time for those closest to you, you're overworked and need to rebalance.

- Friends. As for your friends, if you're pushed for time, plan one larger get together every six to twelve weeks – a cinema trip, a festive meal, a party, a trip to the pub. Twelve week blocks have the advantage of being seasonal. If you don't manage anything else, organise a summer picnic, a Halloween party, a Christmas lunch, and a walk in the woods in the Spring – and at least you've managed to catch up with everyone!

- You and your partner. A great tip someone gave me before we started a family: give each other evenings off (once a fortnight is ideal) and spend one night a week together, even if it's just cuddled up in front of the television.

Think big picture

A bird's eye view

This phrase is a metaphor for a way of thinking about life. Imagine you could hover above the world and see the connections between things: in your own life, the lives of those around you, in your community and in the whole world. In chapter four we talked about contexts: the environment and the people around us affecting our behaviour and the baggage we carry with us through life. These are the things around us that will motivate us to act in a particular way.

Now we're going to look briefly at a different application of the idea: being a divergent thinker.

Convergent and divergent thinkers
In the 1960s, psychologist J.P. Guilford discussed *convergent* thinkers who were able to think accurately and precisely and *divergent* thinkers who could connect a range of different disciplines and come up with multiple creative ideas. It's since been suggested that we tend to do one or the other, that we could be labelled a convergent thinker or a divergent thinker. It's probably more accurate to say that we use both kinds of thinking in different situations but are better at one kind.

A slight adaptation of these ideas describes big picture thinkers who are creative and can make connections between things easily and pits them against details people who are systematic and good at accuracy. Again, it's likely that we do both in different situations but are better at one.

A big picture thinker will have a tendency to over-connect and be surprised by how easily other people seem to compartmentalise. A details person might get so bogged down in detail that they can't see the whole, and may be surprised by how easily others forget to dot 'i's and cross 't's.

When people who are at either ends of the spectrum meet they are likely to find it hard to communicate and may be mystified as to why they can't understand one another. Yet in fact they *need* the other's way of thinking to complement their own. A business will benefit from knowing about and using both ways of thinking equally.

Divergent thinking exercises

When we're looking for a balanced way to manage our time, there's a point at which we need to be systematic and specific about our goals and how to achieve them but also we need to take time to step back and do some big picture thinking. We tried to be as systematic and specific as we could about breaking down our goals into small steps in the first section, and also to look at the impact on our lives as a whole.

1. Now take a moment to apply big picture thinking to *the way you use your time*. Review the activities you did in chapter eleven and imagine you could hover over your life. Imagine you could take the roof off your house or look through the walls and doors. Go out a bit further and imagine you could do the same with your neighbours' houses. Now try your whole street. What about the whole town?
   a. How do you use your time?
   b. Why do you use your time?
   c. Can you spot any extra time you didn't know you had? (How long do you spend waiting in an average week, for instance?)

2. Are you really time-poor? Let's examine your time priorities. Keep in mind the exercises you did during previous chapters in this section and the definitions of 'important' we looked at earlier. Create two lists as follows:
   a. What's the most important thing you need to do today, this week, this month, this year?
   b. What else do you need to get done today, this week, this month, this year?
   c. How balanced are your two lists?

Key points

In this chapter, we've covered:

1. Make it count:
    a. Doing whatever you're doing and being present
    b. Doing the important stuff
    c. Staying task-focused
    d. Flexibility

2. Keep it balanced:
    a. Your year pie chart
    b. What is balanced time management?
    c. THESE and THEM

3. Think big picture
    a. A bird's eye view
    b. Convergent and divergent thinkers
    c. Divergent thinking exercises

****

Chapter 14: Balanced Planning

About this chapter
In this chapter we look at two ways of planning your time: the minute-by-minute approach and a form of timetabling, using morning, afternoon and evening sessions. The chapter finishes with some tips on implementing balanced time management and some exercises to try.

The minute-by-minute approach
There are lots of ways to plan your time. One isn't necessarily better than any other as long as you make it work. Some writers of time management books suggest very specific scheduling, with different sized chunks of time, a bit like this:

7 – 8 get ready for work
8 – 9 drive to work
9 – 9.15 review diary
9.15 – 9.30 answer or flag any urgent emails
9.30 – 10 staff meeting
10 – 10.15 update PA
10.15 – 11 review marketing strategy with Nancy
11 – 11.15 coffee
11.15 – 11.25 call Dave back
11.25 – 11.45 go over report guidelines
11.45 – 12 answer or flag any urgent emails

Phew. I was so exhausted making this up I had to stop and I'd only got to 12! But this approach does have some advantages:

- It is a good way to fit in all your tasks and to prioritise them.

- It's also a good way to use little bits of time that would otherwise be lost.
- If you stuck to your schedule it would make you focus – no more rechecking emails when Dave is expecting your call.
- Scheduling like this is usually more suitable at work than at home and it will help keep work and home separate.
- Even if you have to spend half an hour every day setting it up you'll probably get that time back through efficiency savings.
- If you're working in a team on event management or something complicated or time-bound, you'll probably work like this out of necessity.

So how do you do it?

1. Set up one very detailed Small Steps To Do List to draw from everyday. Add deadlines to it so you know in advance when each task will be completed. Add who's responsible for each task, if appropriate. **There's a to do list template for you to download on the website.**

2. Before you leave work, schedule your tasks for the next day. Some items will always appear – such as 'answer or flag any urgent emails.' Some will be scheduled by others or appear regularly on certain days of the week – such as 'staff meeting'.

3. Give each task a time slot during your day using a diary that's laid out that way or an app on your phone or hand-held device.

4. Allow some time for unexpected tasks that come up during the day.

5. Keep your minute-by-minute schedule handy on your desk so you can see it.

6. At the end of the day review the schedule and plan the next day.

What's wrong with this approach?

- It is exhausting to plan every day in this much detail and it takes time to do the plan
- It is tempting to plan to use every last little bit of time when - if you think about the rhythm of your day - this doesn't always feel right
- It is tempting to underestimate how much time each thing takes just to fit everything in, which is demoralising when you don't get everything done
- You need at least some downtime – a break, a chat with colleague, a walk to stretch you legs
- At the same time as avoiding annoyances, it's possible to miss unexpected but useful deviations or distractions or opportunities
- Sometimes it's better to take the long route

Familiar verses unfamiliar
The more unfamiliar you are with something – a topic, a job, an event you've got to organise – the more carefully, and the more minute-by-minute, you have to plan.

The more familiar you are with something, the more flexible you can be when you plan your time. You can rely on what has become tacit knowledge for you. Remember that it might not be tacit knowledge for people you're dealing with! This mismatch of tacit knowledge can create big communication problems amongst would-be collaborators.

You can test this theory by applying it to anything you know how to do really well. You probably don't have to plan your route to work minute-by-minute anymore but I bet you planned it carefully on your very first day.

Getting a feel for a fixed timeframe
You might have a fixed time period in which to do a task, self-imposed or otherwise. Here are some points to remember:

- Doing something within a fixed timeframe forces you to get a feel for that period of time.
- Don't be surprised when you need to practice getting used to particular time frames.
- Whether you've promised yourself that you'll work on your Latin grammar or your matchstick model village for a hour every evening, or you're training as a teacher and need to write forty-five minute lesson plans, or you need to snatch fifteen minutes to write flash fiction in your coffee break, it will take a while to get used to the shape of that time period. But it WILL come – you just have to practise.

Timetabling

Timetabling is an alternative to minute-by-minute planning. Perhaps because I spend part of my time teaching, the idea of *timetabling* a day appeals to me more than the minute-by-minute schedule. That's why I've already suggested breaking the day into three sessions: morning, afternoon and evening. You then allocate specific tasks to each session. The advantages are:

- It's flexible. If you've scheduled 'work on event with Martha and Harry' on Monday afternoon you can work on any of the specific tasks associated, as long as you know what they are.
- It encourages you to categorise tasks and group them together.

- It doesn't really matter how long each session is. The plan still works.

- Once you start using your timetable, you'll begin to work out how much you can get done during each session, meaning you can tell how much you're likely to get done in future sessions.

- This approach is good for people who are already busy or family members who all have different routines. It's also good for people with a lot to do and a lot of unstructured time, like students or freelancers.

- You can add detailed minute-by-minute scheduling as well in places, if you need it.

- It's easy to adapt for your own and your family's requirements.

- Remember we looked at rhythms of the year? Watch out for peaks and troughs when using this approach.

So how do you do it?

1. Plan together with anyone else involved.

2. Set up a Master Plan and a Small Steps to Do List - or separate lists - for any big projects. Know when any deadlines are and who's doing what. One of the bonus bits gives you a method for creating your Master Plan. Once created, it turns into a to do list!

3. What's your time frame? Think about the rhythm of the year. You might want to plan in six week blocks, for example, or change the plan with the seasons – or school terms - roughly every twelve weeks. In other words, the whole family gets a timetable for the term or half term.

4. Divide your week into sessions. State roughly what you'll be doing in each session. Do a separate plan for work if you need one.
5. Write it up somewhere you can see it - a white board is ideal.

Using a visual reminder

When you write it up, you can leave space for any specific tasks for particular days or weeks. That's why a whiteboard works so well. Make your timetable big enough and you can fit the whole family on! Everyone gets big a reminder of what they and everyone else are doing – no more "but I told you I was going in to the office today" - and you can tell at a glance what eating arrangements will need to be for that day. You can see that X will need a packed lunch on Tuesday, Wednesday and Thursday and that Friday will need to be a pizza night because you've planned spend the evening buying all your Christmas presents online.

The mini version

You may not need to plan your whole day flexibly. You can use a mini-version of the timetabling approach to plan morning, afternoon and evening sessions to spend working on your goals. Imagine you're arranging a date with yourself and write it in your diary. By the way, arranging one appointment with yourself per week is better than unrealistically committing to every evening after work.

What's wrong with this approach?

- It could become so flexible that you either skip sessions or forget some important tasks. Avoid this by keeping your to do list somewhere you can see it, or checking it regularly.

- It makes it much easier to bring work home. If you often work from home then this is an advantage. If you're trying to leave work in the office then you may need to be strict with yourself.
- It makes it easier to 'waste' time – if you're a procrastinator maybe precise scheduling would work better for you - but on the other hand you might find that you get into a rhythm and any downtime is actually necessary.
- It's possible to be too general. While it's fine to be pretty general with the session title, you do need to get more specific – in ways this book has already described – when allocating individual tasks. Keep to do lists as specific as possible.

Small steps to balanced time management
Planning
Anything big coming up? Having a baby, returning to work, starting a new job, even Christmas or a holiday all have an impact on your planning. We tend to get the sense that we're working towards what will be a break or a new beginning in our lives, and it's hard to see beyond this point. Build in some discussion time to plan for big things in your weekly schedule. Try to look beyond them too. Here are some more quick tips to help you with whichever planning technique you chose:

- Don't hide your plan. Stick it up on the wall or keep it open on your desk.
- Use a calendar as well for any scheduled tasks and big events, especially if several people are involved.
- Review your to do list with anyone else involved once a week.
- Dividing household tasks fairly makes everyone happier.

- Plan for balance. Remember THESE and THEM when you're planning.
- When thinking about your goals, make any extra tasks you've added part of your routine as soon as possible.

Doing

You've planned for balance. You've thought about the rhythm of the year. You've thought carefully about your goals. Now you've scheduled, stick to it:

- The Pomodoro technique works well, even for mundane tasks like vacuuming the lounge, or cleaning the bathroom. It's also good for tasks you're dreading or anything you find it hard to start. Breaks are built in too and full details are available online for free.
- Part of the balanced approach means being balanced in the doing, too. Take breaks, go with the rhythm of the day, stop for a chat or a drink of water, go for a walk.

Reviewing

Check in with yourself and with your family and work colleagues that the way you've arranged your time is working. Don't get into analysis paralysis: checking once every six to twelve weeks works well.

- How much progress did you make towards your goals – the big life goals or the more everyday ones? How much THESE and THEM did you include?
- A food, exercise or sleep diary helps with THESE where there's a particular issue.
- Me-management. Use your journal to record the progress of particular projects and this includes how you're managing your time. For instance, pick just one day. List the things you've managed to achieve, and feel good about it. Writing

them down makes you realise just how much you've done, rather than berating yourself for what you haven't done. If it didn't go so well, you can record the reasons you were interrupted: comfort eating, calls from relatives, trips to the shops, the printer running out of ink – naming what got in the way will help you to adjust your plans.

Balanced planning on trial

Try these exercises:

If you're unconvinced, then experiment with each approach as follows.

- First create a Master Plan and Small Steps To Do List if you haven't done so already.
- Have a go at planning in minute-by-minute detail for one day. If the approach works for you, extend for a week.
- Have a go at timetabling – giving each morning, afternoon and evening a general title or theme – for one day. If the approach works for you, extend for a week.

Key Points

In this chapter we've covered:

1. Detailed scheduling
2. Timetabling
3. Using a visual reminder
4. Small steps to balanced time management: planning, doing, reviewing
5. Balanced planning on trial

****

Chapter 15: Small Adjustments

About this chapter

Small adjustments are small things you can do differently in your day-to-day life that allow you to manage your time better. I suggest you read through this chapter and then spend some time creating a good filing system, before setting up some more systems and routines that work for you. Then make regular admin part of your week. If you are completely snowed under by admin tasks and bits of paper and don't know where to start, I recommend adopting David Allen's approach from his book *Getting Things Done*. There's more in the resources section. The final sections of this chapter focus on money and stuff, with some practical tips to help you sort them out!

Admin

Your own PA

So what do I mean by admin? In this context, admin is doing whatever it takes to run your life, like acting as your own PA. You can also use admin time to manage your goals. Be your own PA with the three Rs of small steps admin.

1. Regular. Manage your admin tasks – keep a list of them - at least once a week. Often these are financial matters or to do with the place where you live or running your household.
   a. Remember to break it down and make it easy.
   b. Meet weekly with your partner or the whole family to discuss running the household.

      c. Create a folder and a list of admin tasks related to one of your goals.

2. Reduce. Decide which tasks need doing and which are unimportant. Keep chipping away at your list and at your filing.

      a. Do you really need to keep all of those pieces of paper?

      b. Make the papers you need regularly easy to find and use.

3. Recycle – don't hoard. Sometimes filing can be an excuse for not letting go. Recycle it instead. Make recycling part of your admin.

      a. De-junk and clear the clutter. (See chapter twelve).

      b. Create a space for recycling and learn how to recycle confidential information.

Systems and routines

Become a system-addict

You can, and probably already do, use systems and routines at home and at work. Some of these might be subconscious, habitual ways of working. Some are more conscious. As we're looking at small things you can do differently to manage your time better, the aim is to become more conscious of the systems and routines we use.

- A system is a pre-planned way of doing or organising something.
- A routine is a pre-planned way of structuring your day or part of it, or another period of time: a week, a term, a year.

Semi-flexible, simple or straightforward, and shared

Creating a system or routine or re-evaluating existing ones can help a great deal with time management. For this to work, your systems and routines need to be:

- Semi-flexible. "Semi" because you don't *constantly* reinvent yourself, or give in to others who want to override you, and "flexible" because you don't carry on stubbornly when something *needs* to change.
- Simple or straightforward. You need to be able to remember it and make it habitual. Yes, you can write it out or stick it on the wall but don't make it too complicated. If you can't simplify the different aspects that make up your system or routine then at least make your plan easy to follow. Write yourself some instructions. If a task involves something stressful or difficult, avoid multi-tasking.
- Shared with anyone who needs to know. If you've got a great idea for making your children's bedtime routine easier, talk to your partner about it. Keeping it to yourself won't make things better.

So how do you do it?

I discovered very quickly that, after giving love and providing for your child's basic needs, the most important thing you can do as a parent is *anticipate*. It's good advice for time management purposes too. To create a new system or routine:

1. Think ahead to what you need to do.
2. Set it up.
3. Break it down into small steps.
4. Make it easy.
5. Anticipate interruptions or other demands that might be made on your time. Be as specific as you can when designing your system or routine. Use twelve week chunks of time and consider the peaks and troughs in your year.

Examples systems and routines

Here are some examples of the kinds of systems and routines you could invent at home and at work:

- A way of filing your notes alphabetically so you can access them easily.
- A way of laying out your room to make the most of the space.
- A cooking and shopping rota cross-listed with an online shopping list, designed to save money by helping you use up all the food you buy.
- A laundry routine that includes a system for sorting the laundry as you put it in the laundry basket and a system to make it easy to put away clean clothes.
- A way to make sure everyone in the team shares their ideas.
- A way to make sure everyone knows which meetings take place when and where.
- A system for communicating to managers the small things that would improve the working environment.
- A way to make sure every child in the class walks to school once a week.
- A bedtime routine for your children that allows you and your partner one night off a week.

Filing

Your Filing System

This section is inspired by an Oliver Burkeman column called 'The Joy of Filing' where he points out that "almost all filing systems are [...] pointlessly laborious" and suggests "a middle way". Have a look in the resources section if you'd like to read it.

It took me a very long time to work out how to make filing work. I had three problems, which I've since learnt are common exasperators:

- Keeping unnecessary bits of paper
- Maintaining a system that's too complicated to use easily
- Forgetting (or losing) something when it's filed

I discovered that the answer (as it is with lots of things) is to keep it as simple as possible. Reducing the pile of papers by recycling and filing everything alphabetically solved the problem of losing things. So remember to keep things simple and make it easy to use!

Practical help with your filing dilemmas

Let's be blunt, this is a system you need to set up straight away. If you need filing help, try this:

1. Put aside plenty of time to work on your filing.
2. Get hold of some box files. Using box files means you can take out a file and look for what you need. It keeps your papers tidy. It is also possible to keep them on a shelf if you need to.
3. Put everything into alphabetical order. 'Alphabetical' is of course open to interpretation. Do the cats' vaccination records go under V for vet or C for cat or P for pet? Do credit card statements go under C for credit card or B for bills or do you go by the name of the company? I suggest being consistent and sticking to the company name. Alternatively go with whatever comes to you first when you think about it – because hopefully you'll file it where you'll end up looking for it!
4. Have one box file dedicated to papers that need to be easy for someone else to find in a difficult situation, such as details of home and life insurance and wills.

5. Any big project with lots of papers associated can have a box file to itself or a whole filing cabinet if you need it.

6. As you put everything into alphabetical order, create a recycling pile for anything you don't need. Use a third 'not sure' pile to review later to avoid a long decision making process.

7. Use one of the box files for miscellaneous bits such as interesting articles, places to visit and postcards. Consider what it says in chapter 13 about the non-important non-urgent stuff.

8. Use the other box files to divide and file your papers alphabetically.

9. Recycle the papers you don't need. Do this securely.

10. Ideally keep the box files in a lockable, fireproof filing cabinet. If that's not possible, keep important papers, insurance documents and wills in a secure fireproof box.

Make your filing easy

Once your system is set up, you need to use it. To make it easy, I suggest:

1. Keeping a filing, pending and action file in easy reach. Inside a desk drawer is ideal.

2. Keeping a small indoor recycling box or bag somewhere easy to get to. Empty it regularly.

3. Making filing part of your admin time each week.

4. Keep a separate ongoing miscellaneous file in easy reach if you have trouble making decisions about whether to throw something out. Put the things you don't know what to do with in here and review them every so often.

5. You might also like a folder for particular items in easy reach on a bookshelf or in a kitchen drawer. For example, vouchers or money off coupons, info on days out, recipes,

letters from your kids' school. Treat this folder like a book you use every day.

Money
Saving time and money
Money can be a real time waster in and of itself, so can worrying about money. Facing up to how you feel about money and dealing with what needs to be done, step by step, could save you a fortune as well as saving you time each week.

Deal with it
Sorting out your money is an important part of admin or being your own PA. Many of us have to sort out our relationship with money too. Many of us have our head in the sand when it comes to our debts. If that includes you, take a small step towards sorting it out today. Face it and work out a way to deal with it and it becomes a whole lot less scary. Do this regularly during your admin time.

Plan it
Dealing with money isn't just about how you might use money on a day-to-day basis or how to budget or pay off your debts. Planning it puts you in control and again makes it less scary. Again, use small steps. Money admin involves planning:

- for events that take place every year like birthdays and Christmas
- to save money by sticking to a budget and following money saving advice
- for the financial side of your goals
- for big life events like university, weddings and funerals
- for your long term future

Plan it: an example

Managing your everyday spending and limiting your trips to the shops is a good way to stop impulse buys. Save money and time by using the following small steps:

- Buy a pack of greetings cards to send out and keep them in date order (by family member's birthday).
- When something you use regularly (not something you don't) is on special offer, buy enough for the year if you can afford it and have a place to store it.
- If you send a lot of post, consider buying stamps in one go at the beginning of the year. You can beat any price rise this way and avoid trips to the shops where you'll come back with a bag full!
- Have fruit and veg delivered to avoid impulse buys at the supermarket.

Understand it

This is beyond the scope of this book but another fear-reducing strategy is simply to understand money better. You can do that by talking to a financial advisor, going on a personal finances course, asking for more training at work, brushing up on your maths skills at the local library and reading one of the books in the resources section.

Stuff

Throughout this chapter on small adjustments, you might have noticed a theme. In fact it's a theme that runs right through this book. You're aiming to simplify and to make life easier and one way to do it is by reducing and recycling. The same principles apply to stuff.

Use it

We've looked at niggles and bugs, but what if you did the opposite? What if you did a survey of all your stuff and make a note of the things that you use regularly that you really love? What would come out top? Things are useful and it's not always the most expensive things either! We're often told on the one hand that liking stuff is bad and on the other hand – by advertisers everywhere – that we should buy more stuff. This is one way to work your way out of that particular paradox:

- Show some appreciation for the things you use a lot.
- Know what you would do if they went wrong.
- Save for a replacement.
- Know where the manual is kept.
- Make them as easy to use as possible.

Treasure it

There are some things we like because they are precious to us. Because of their monetary value, because of the memories they hold for us, just because we happen to like tea towels or old coins. We know that we can't take it with us, but we'll enjoy it while we can.

Don't feel like you have to get rid of your collection of thimbles or nineteenth century kaleidoscopes just because you don't use them every day. Ask yourself honestly if this is a hobby you're keeping up for the sake of it, but allow yourself to enjoy the things you treasure just because, too. Some things you'll want to pass on to your loved ones. Specify it in your will and make sure they are safe and stored adequately.

Display it

If you have room, try displaying the items you treasure. Protect them with a display case or plastic covering as appropriate.

Donate it

There are charities waiting to take things you don't need off your hands. Charity shops are a starting point. There are also specialist charities that will take away unwanted furniture and give it to families who need it.

Swap it

If you know likeminded people well enough, you could start your own swapping group. Alternatively, there are swap events and swap shops springing up in towns and cities where you can take your stuff.

Recycle or give it away

Most towns have a recycling centre where you can take unwanted stuff – and it's not just paper and tins they want these days. There will often be a bin for clothes, shoes and books too. Supermarkets also have similar. Join the growing band of online recyclers and give and receive stuff on freecycle or freegle. Join up, post up your item and someone will take it off your hands.

Sell it

There are several ways to sell unwanted stuff, with online marketplaces opening this route up to almost everyone. Here are the main ways to sell:

- Use gumtree, ebay, amazon or one of the other online selling points.
- Car boot sales.
- Specialist markets.
- Nearly new sales.

Key points
In this chapter, we've covered:

1. Admin
   - Be your own PA
   - The 3 'Rs' of small steps admin: Regular, Reduce, Recycle
2. Systems and routines
   - Become a system-addict
   - Semi-flexible, simple or straightforward, and shared
   - So how do you do it?
   - Examples systems and routines
3. Filing
   - Your Filing System
   - Practical help with your filing dilemmas
   - Make your filing easy
4. Money
   - Saving time and money
   - Deal with it
   - Plan it
   - Plan it: an example
   - Understand it
5. Stuff
   - Use it
   - Treasure it
   - Display it
   - Donate it
   - Swap it
   - Recycle or freecyle it
   - Sell it

****

Chapter 16: Small Tools

About this chapter
This short chapter gives you small steps and tips to use when it comes to the tools we use in life everyday. It covers basic tools (seemingly too trivial to organise but actually a real annoyance-saver), making your computer work for you, and another look at your niggles and bugs and your grateful list.

Focus on the small stuff
Basic tools and small annoyances
Basic tools are very easy to overlook, or to dismiss as trivial, but essential to the small steps method. Keys, pens, notebooks, anything you use a lot could be a basic tool. If you've been working on the exercises throughout, you'll have done similar exercises to this one already. Spend a day being aware of any small annoyances. This time focus on basic tools that you use everyday.

- *"I can never find my keys."*
- *"None of the pens in the pot work."*
- *"I missed J's parent's evening because I lost the letter."*
- *"My pillow's uncomfortable."*
- *"The recycling looks ugly."*
- *"I forget to take my pills."*
- *"I'm supposed to file my receipts somewhere."*
- *"The phone wire keeps getting tangled."*

What can you do about it?
There are small steps all of the respondents above could take to save themselves time everyday and to stop feeling annoyed. Tools that can help with the niggles above include:

1. A key basket or pot
2. Several notebooks and (working) pens
3. A pin board / whiteboard / family calendar
4. Have good look at your sleeping area – which of your sleeping tools work for you and which don't?
5. A small-enough-to-hide recycling tub for indoors and a recycling system that's part of your daily routine.
6. A kid-safe see-through box to keep pills out of harm's way but in view. Or a pill drawer that's very near to something you access all the time – like the fridge or your computer table.
7. A key basket or pot could collect receipts as you come in the door. Or keep an envelope handy nearby.
8. A cordless phone!

The grateful list revisited.

Early on in this book I suggested stopping for a moment every so often and jotting down the things you are grateful for right now. If the small annoyances exercise has left you feeling deflated, try spending a day carrying a notebook and recording things you are grateful for. It has a powerful effect!

Get digital

Making your computer work for you.

A computer is a fantastic tool. You can use it for research, shopping, communication, record keeping, journaling, photography and even build a small business using it. If you need to develop your I.T. skills there are plenty of course around. If you're already pretty I.T. savvy, challenge yourself to expand your comfort zone. Learn how to do something you've never done before. Whatever your skill level you can save time by making your computer work for you:

- Look at your weekly routine. Can you identify anything that could be done better or more efficiently using a computer *even if you would need to learn new skills?*
- In chapter eleven you identified peaks and troughs in your year. Look at your year again and ask the same question. Over the year, can you identify anything that could be done better or more efficiently using a computer *even if you would need to learn new skills?*

Online tools
Some of the resources mentioned in this book include online tools. Here are some of the ones you can use to help with balanced time management.

- Freecycle, freegle - or other recycling / swap sites
- ebay and Amazon or other online selling sites
- Skills swap websites

Digital timewasting?
As with any addictive habit, online activity can become a time waster. You can either limit your time online so that you get as much time in the real world as possible, by using the Pomodoro technique, or go the other way and immerse yourself, running your life through your online connections, using it to your advantage as much as possible.

Is your computer a time-sucker?
Is your computer sucking the time out of your life? Because a computer is such a fantastic tool it is worth getting it to run as efficiently as possible, by making sure you have the skills needed,

but also by sorting out the niggles. Do the niggle exercise again but this time, focus on your computer and your use of the internet. Here are some common niggles:

- *"My computer takes ages to load up."*
- *"My internet service keeps cutting out."*
- *"I don't know how to X and don't know how to find the answer."*
- *"My computer annoys me."*

De-niggle your computer

There are small steps all of the respondents above could take to save themselves time. Tools that can help with the computer-based niggles above include:

1. Removing some of the applications and programmes that start up when your computer starts up. (Get some technical advice on this one!)

2. Make sure you're on the right package by phoning your provider and compare providers using one of the price comparison websites. Some rural communities are starting their own local service providers. Consider your current download allowance and maximum broadband speed.

3. There are some things that we know we don't know. If you know you don't know how to do something on your computer, you can identify the small steps to take to find out how.

   - Try the 'help menu' if it's a computer programme.
   - Use a search engine to find out.
   - Try your local library.
   - There are some friendly magazines on the market which don't assume too much basic knowledge.
   - Find someone who will sit next to you and go through step-by-step.

Are you missing out?
A while back I used to help beginners learn more about computing and the internet. Many people were eager to learn how to shop online or stay in touch with their family. However, I noticed that some people found computers intensely annoying, were cynical about every move, almost like they were playing chess with a machine, or worried about pressing or clicking on the wrong thing. Usually when they had learnt some basic I.T. skills the suspicion was gone, but for some it hung on. On the other hand, some people have been familiar with computers from an early age but still find them faintly annoying. Fine, everyone has an impatience button somewhere! But computers can help to such an extent that you could be missing out. If this sounds like you, ask yourself *why?* Once you know why you can take some small steps towards doing something about it.

- Is it that the room with the computer in it is cold / noisy / damp / a cupboard?
- Is it that it's not running fast enough?
- Is there something you want to make it do, but can't?

Looking back on your niggles and bugs
The niggles and bugs exercises revisited
We've done the niggles and bugs exercise in different ways throughout this book. I've treated niggles as small, specific annoyances – perhaps at the back of the mind – and bugs as more general and random. I suggest that you repeat these regularly, doing the positive and the negative versions of this exercise perhaps a couple of times a year. Here they are again:
1. Write down every small niggle that annoys you, interrupts you, frustrates you or prevents you from doing what you want to do. Create some small steps to do something about any niggle that's in your control.

2. Keep a bugs diary. Note *anything at all* that bugs you. Create some small steps to help you to de-bug anything in your control.
3. Do a survey of all your stuff, making a note of the things that you use regularly *that you really love.*
4. Note small annoyances, focusing on *basic tools* that you use everyday.
5. Do the niggle exercise again but this time, focus on your computer and your use of the internet.
6. Early on in the book you wrote a grateful list. Later you did a grateful list specifically about the people in your life.

What happens next?

When you review these exercises again and again – including your grateful lists - a funny thing happens:

- After a time most of the niggles and bugs in your notebook don't matter any more.
- Some of the niggles and bugs will have become so habitual you've forgotten there's another way to do it.
- One or two may stand out to such an extent that you can no longer ignore them.
- The lists of things you love will either prove that something *wasn't* as useful as you thought it was, or it will help you appreciate the enduring usefulness of whatever it is.
- The grateful lists will make you smile and provide inspiration and encouragement as well as helping you put the niggles and bugs in perspective.

Key points
In this chapter we've covered:
1. Focus on the small stuff

- Basic tools and small annoyances
- What can you do about it?
- The grateful list revisited.

2. Get digital
   - Making your computer work for you.
   - Online tools
   - Digital timewasting?
   - Is your computer a time-sucker?
   - De-niggle your computer
   - Are you missing out?

3. Looking back on your niggles and bugs
   - The niggles and bugs exercises revisited
   - What happens next?

The final two chapters provide you with small ways to keep in check and a list of helpful resources.

············

Chapter 17: Small Ways to Keep Check

About this chapter

In the opening chapter I gave you some small ways to keep tabs on your progress and promised you some more. Well, here they are! This short chapter summarises five main ways to keep in check: check in, communicate, collaborate, collect and compost. Use any of these techniques to regularly review, monitor and evaluate your progress, while making a record in your notebook or your journal. As with all the exercises in this book, only use those that appeal to you.

Check in

Make a date with yourself

Every so often make a date with yourself. Go somewhere by yourself or simply spend time doing nothing by yourself. If you want to read more about this idea, have a look at Julia Cameron's work. I review one of her books briefly in chapter seven.

Make it regular

If you've decided to set goals for yourself, if you've decided to manage time differently, then it is worth going over your goals regularly, even if you can only manage once a month.

Remind yourself

Find at least three ways to remind yourself of the goals you've set or the time management strategies you want to try. For example:

- Put it in view in more than once place: the fridge, calendar, noticeboard or whiteboard.
- Block out space in your diary.
- Use a reminder on your phone or hand-held device.

Set it up in advance
In the heat of the moment it's very difficult to stick to what we've decided to do. Instead set up a way of doing it in advance and stick to it. Even better, make it habitual.

Remember to make it easy.
The easier you make the process, the more likely you are to do it. Make your steps small enough so that they seem simple enough to achieve. If in doubt set yourself one task, achievable in one session (morning, evening or afternoon) and that could be built into your day.

Communicate
Talk to others, talk to yourself
Remember to communicate your ideas, worries, questions and thought processes about your goals and your new time management strategies. Partly we do this because negotiating with and understanding others is important to the process, partly because saying something out loud or writing it down is a way of thinking. It's also a way of communicating with yourself. You can do this by:

- Discussing ideas informally: make time to chat when the pressure is off and without applying any pressure yourself.
- Holding meetings: bring the interested parties together, use an agenda and create a list of action points, with deadlines. Make sure everyone is heard.
- Teaching: teaching others about something means you end up explaining it to yourself! You'll also learn about the subject as your research it for your students.
- Journaling: the process of writing a journal allows you to communicate how you really feel about something and allows your brain the space to come up with some solutions to problems.

- Blogging: the digital equivalent to journaling, although (unless you keep it under a password) anyone can read it. Any kind of writing process will help you to iron out the whys and wherefores of an issue, on or off line.
- Emailing and messaging: Make the most of your digital world, including social networking and email, to communicate with a wide range of people.

Collaborate

Groups get you going.

Previously we talked about the importance of support when planning to achieve your goals. Collaboration with others is also a good way to keep check. Groups are motivating. You can provide support to others and they can support you. This works for direct support (like a Quit Smoking group) or indirect support (the friendship provided by a club or society). Collaborating with a group of people on your project will provide a number of people to call you up any time your progress stalls.

When you have *to collaborate*

When thinking about your goals and the ways in which you manage your time, you might *want to* collaborate but you might also *have to* collaborate with any of the following people:

- your partner
- your family
- your friends
- your colleagues
- fellow students

It's therefore worth finding out more about working in a team and group dynamics and I suggest some resources in the final chapter. After all, their success affects *your* success. Collaboration can make you happy, too. Teamwork is included in the list of key character strengths developed by Positive Psychologists.

Collect
The collecting process
Another small way to keep in check is to make time to collect together any of the following. Collect them together in a box file, scrapbook or on a noticeboard. The process of collecting these things together keeps you thinking about and reviewing your progress. Remember the section on confirmation bias? You see what you focus on!

- information
- equipment
- articles
- images
- noticeboard items: either inspirational or practical ones

Compost
Garden time revisited
I've already said that sometimes working toward your goals is like gardening. It takes time to make a garden. Preparing the ground, putting in your plants and tending them as they grow takes years not minutes. When you've researched what it takes to achieve your goals, when you've thought about the changes you can make to manage time more effectively, give it time, especially if you want a particular technique to become second nature. Give yourself time to:

- let it sink in
- let it mature

It may seem as though only the passing of time can allow this to happen, but you can deliberately leave things to compost by taking time out, going on walks, spending time with those you love, or doing things with your hands if you usually work with your head. It helps if you combine this kind of composting with journaling.

Key points
In this chapter, we've covered:

1. Check in
   - Make a date with yourself
   - Make it regular
   - Remind yourself
   - Set it up in advance
   - Remember to make it easy.
2. Communicate
   - discussion
   - meetings
   - teaching
   - journaling
   - blogging
   - emailing
3. Collaborate
   - Groups get you going.
   - When you *have* to collaborate
4. Collect
   - information
   - equipment
   - articles
   - images
   - noticeboard items
5. Compost
   - let it sink in
   - let it mature

Chapter 18: Bibliography and Resources

This chapter includes:

- A list of bonus bits and direction to more help on the smallstepsguide.co.uk website.
- A list of books and websites to refer to if you want more on a particular issue or topic.
- A list of websites to help with some of the topics raised in the book.
- A list of the books and websites referred chapter by chapter.

Bonus bits:

You can download the following bonus bits from the Small Steps website at www.smallstepsguide.co.uk The password is 'polarbears'.

- ready-made goals chart
- two example flowcharts
- using a search engine
- Small Steps To Do List template
- an example of timetabling
- Maslow's Hierarchy and small adjustments
- How to create the Small Steps Master Plan
- Small Steps Master Plan template for creating one

Resources

Here are some books and articles to read if you'd like to find out more about a particular topic. Many fit into more than one category.

Goal Setting

- Ditzler, Jinny, *Your Best Year Yet: Make the Next 12 Months Your Best Ever* (Harper Element) 2006

Happiness

- Ricard, Matthieu, *The Art of Happiness: A Guide to Developing Life's Most Important Skill* (Atlantic) 2007
- Lyubomirsky, Sonja, *The How Of Happiness: A Practical Guide to Getting The Life You Want* (Piatkus) 2010
- Haidt, Jonathan, *The Happiness Hypothesis: Putting Ancient Wisdom to the Test of Modern Science* (Arrow) 2007

Money

- Hall, Alvin, *Your Money or Your Life: A Practical Guide to Managing and Improving Your Financial Life* (Atria) 2009
- Lowe, Jonquil, *Be Your Own Financial Adviser: The Comprehensive Guide to Wealth and Financial Planning* (Prentice Hall) 2010
- Middleton, J., *Detox Your Finances: 52 Brilliant Ideas for Personal Finance Success* (Infinite Ideas) 2007
- Pine, Karen J., and Gnessen, Simonne, *Sheconomics* (Headline) 2009

Motivation and effectiveness

- Covey, Stephen R., *The 7 Habits of Highly Effective People* (Simon and Schuster) 2004. (See page 288 for reference to our "physical", "mental", "spiritual" and "social / emotional" needs.)
- Kelsey, Robert, *What's Stopping You? Why Smart People Don't Always Reach Their Potential and How You Can* (Capstone) 2011

- Tschäppeler, Roman, *The Decision Book: Fifty Models for Strategic Thinking* (Profile) 2011
- Burkeman, Oliver, *Help: How to Become Slightly Happier and Get a Bit More Done* (Cannongate) 2011

Organisation and Productivity
- Allen, David, *Getting Things Done: How to Achieve Stress-free Productivity* (Piatkus) 2002. Website: http://www.davidco.com/about-gtd
- Eisenberg, Ronni, *Organise Yourself* (Piatkus) 2006
- Leeds, Regina, *One Year to an Organized Life: From Your Closets to Your Finances* (Da Capo Lifelong) 2008

Success, failure and practice
- Dweck, Carol S., *Mindset: How You Can Fulfil Your Potential* (Robinson) 2012
- Gladwell, Malcolm, *Outliers: The Story of Success* (Penguin) 2009
- Harford, Tim, *Adapt: Why Success Always Starts with Failure* (Abacus) 2011
- Syed, Matthew, *Bounce: The Myth of Talent and the Power of Practice* (Fourth Estate) 2011

Thinking creatively: Tony Buzan
- Buzan, Tony, *Use Your Head: How to Unleash the Power of Your Mind* (BBC Active) 2010
- Buzan, Tony, *The Mind Map Book: Unlock Your Creativity, Boost Your Memory, Change Your Life* (BBC Active) 2009.
- Buzan, Tony, *The Power of Creative Intelligence: 10 ways to Tap Into Your Creative Genius* (Thorsons) 2001: website: http://www.thinkbuzan.com/uk/

Time management

- Cirillo, Francesco *The Pomodoro Technique* (Lulu.com) 2009 Available to download for free from: www.pomodorotechnique.com
- Forster, Mark, *Do it Tomorrow and Other Secrets of Time Management* (Hodder and Stoughton) 2006 and *Get Everything Done and Still Have Time to Play* (Hodder and Stoughton) 2000. See: www.markforster.net
- Mackenzie, R. Alec, *The Time Trap: The Classic Book on Time Management* (McGraw-Hill) 1975

Writing a journal

- 'Getting into Writing', in Bolton, Gillie, Field, Victoria, and Thompson, Kate, *Writing Routes: A Resource Handbook of Therapeutic Writing* (Jessica Kingsley Publishers) 2010, pages 17 – 34
- Cameron, Julia, *The Artist's Way* (Pan) 2011
- Cameron, Julia, *The Sound of Paper* (Penguin) 2006. Website: http://juliacameronlive.com

Websites
Online selling sites
www.gumtree.com
www.ebay.co.uk
www.amazon.co.uk

Recycling / freebie sites
http://www.sofaproject.org.uk/about-us.html
www.ilovefreegle.org
http://uk.freecycle.org/
For a list of other sites, scroll to the bottom of the following page:
http://www.moneysavingexpert.com/shopping/freecycle

Skills exchange
www.swapaskill.com/about
http://skillsexchange.net/skills/general/about.html

Volunteering
Timebank: http://timebank.org.uk/who-we-are
Do it! www.do-it.org.uk
UK Volunteering: www.ukvolunteering.org
Volunteering England:
www.volunteering.org.uk/iwanttovolunteer/where-do-i-start
Volunteering Northern Ireland: www.nidirect.gov.uk/find-voluntary-work-in-the-uk
Volunteering Scotland:
www.volunteerscotland.org.uk/WantToVolunteer/
Volunteering Wales: www.volunteering-wales.net

Books, articles and ideas I've mentioned, by chapter
Chapter 1
- Cameron, Julia, *The Artist's Way* (Pan) 2011
- Cameron, Julia, *The Sound of Paper* (Penguin) 2006
- Maslow, Abraham, 'A theory of human motivation', *Psychological Review,* No. 50, 1943, pages 370-96. For more on Maslow's Hierarchy of Needs see Atkinson, Sam et al, eds., *The Psychology Book,* (Dorling Kindersly) 2012, p. 138 – 139.

Chapter 2
- Weak contacts. Have a look at Christakis, Nicholas and Fowler, James 'The Strength of Weak Ties' in *Connected: The Amazing Power of Social Networks and How They Shape Our Lives* (Harper Press) 2011, pp. 156 – 163.

Chapter 3: Goal-setting

- Eisenberg, Ronni, *Organise Yourself* (Piatkus) 2006
- Forster, Mark, *Do it Tomorrow and Other Secrets of Time Management* (Hodder and Stoughton) 2006 and *Get Everything Done and Still Have Time to Play* (Hodder and Stoughton) 2000. Website: www.markforster.net
- Guardian Magazine, Saturday 5th May 2012: www.guardian.co.uk/theguardian/2012/may/05/weekend
- The Pomodoro Technique website: www.pomodorotechnique.com

Chapter 4: What it takes to get where you want to go

- Confirmation bias and cognitive dissonance. See: Winstanley, Julie, *Key Concepts in Psychology* (Palgrave) 2006 and Colman, Andrew, *A Dictionary of Psychology* (Oxford Reference) 2009. You can see a list of cognitive biases online at: http://en.wikipedia.org/wiki/List_of_cognitive_biases
- Water Aid website: www.wateraid.org/uk/about_us/default.asp
- Weak contacts. Have a look at Christakis, Nicholas and Fowler, James 'The Strength of Weak Ties' in *Connected: The Amazing Power of Social Networks and How They Shape Our Lives* (Harper Press) 2011, pp. 156 – 163.
- 'Woman gives birth hours after running Chicago Marathon', *BBC News website*, 11th October 2011 www.bbc.co.uk/news/world-us-canada-15251624

Chapter 5: Reality check

- The Alcoholic's Prayer (or Serenity Prayer) was attributed to Reinhold Niebuhr in Sifton, Elisabeth, *The Serenity Prayer: Faith and Politics in Times of Peace and War* (Norton) 2004.

- Arvon Foundation is a charity providing writing courses and retreats: http://www.arvonfoundation.org
- The commitment quotation comes from Murray, W. H., *The Scottish Himalayan Expedition* (Dent) 1951.

Chapter 6: The Pursuit of Happiness
Autonomy:

- Nauert, Rick, 'Happiness Tied to Choice and Autonomy, Not Money', Psych Central, June 2011. http://psychcentral.com/news/2011/06/15/some-items-more-important-than-money-for-happiness/26945.html
- Salmansohn, Karen, 'The No. 1 Contributor to Happiness: Why/how to regain your autonomy to increase your joy!' *Psychology Today website*, 2011. www.psychologytoday.com/blog/bouncing-back/201106/the-no-1-contributor-happiness

Ed Diener:

- Biswas-Diener, Robert and Diener, Ed, *Happiness: Unlocking the Mysteries of Psychological Wealth* (Wiley-Blackwell) 2008
- Rudin, Mike, 'The science of happiness', *BBC News website*, 2006 http://news.bbc.co.uk/1/hi/programmes/happiness_formula/4783836.stm
- Wallis, Claudia, 'The Science of Happiness Turns 10. What has it taught?' *Time Magazine*, 2009 www.time.com/time/health/article/0,8599,1908173,00.htm

Happiness measures:

- Better Life Index. The OECD's Better Life Index is at: http://oecdbetterlifeindex.org/about/better-life-initiative/ (OECD stands for the Organisation for Economic Co-operation and Development.)

- GNH. Several books on happiness mention Gross National Happiness or GNH. For example, Anielski, Mark, *The Economics of Happiness: Building Genuine Wealth* (New Society) 2007.
- UK Happiness Index:
  - o Office for National Statistics, 'Initial investigation into Subjective Well-being from the Opinions Survey' ONS website, 1st December 2011 http://tinyurl.com/ONSwellbeingsurvey
  - o Rogers, Simon, 'Happiness index: how happy are you and David Cameron?' Guardian website, 1st December 2011 http://www.guardian.co.uk/news/datablog/2011/dec/01/happiness-index-david-cameron

Positive psychology:
- Positive psychology website: http://www.ppc.sas.upenn.edu/faqs.htm
- Seligman, Martin E.P., *Flourish: A Visionary New Understanding of Happiness and Well-being* (Nicholas Brealey) 2011
- Seligman, Martin E.P., *Authentic Happiness: Using the New Positive Psychology to Realise Your Potential for Lasting Fulfilment* (Nicholas Brealey) 2003
- Seligman's website: http://www.authentichappiness.sas.upenn.edu

Teams, social dynamics and altruism:
- Brown, Michael, Brown, R Stephanie L., Penner, Louis A., *Moving Beyond Self-Interest: Perspectives from Evolutionary Biology, Neuroscience, and the Social Sciences*, OUP USA, 2011

- Christakis, Nicholas and Fowler, James *Connected: The Amazing Power of Social Networks and How They Shape Our Lives* (Harper Press) 2011
- Lewis, Sarah, *Positive Psychology at Work: How Positive Leadership and Appreciative Inquiry Create Inspiring Organizations* (Wiley-Blackwell) 2011

Chapter 7: A review of goal setting methods, including the no-goal method

Productivity, work or sales:

- Johnson, Spencer, *Who Moved My Cheese: An Amazing Way to Deal with Change in Your Work and in Your Life* (Vermilion) 1999. See: www.whomovedmycheese.com
- Tracey, Brian, *Goals: How to Get Everything You Want Faster Than You Ever Thought Possible* (Berrett-Koehler) 2010
- Ziglar, Zig, *Top Performance: How to Develop Excellence in Yourself and Others* (Revell) 2004

Success:

- Covey, Stephen, *The 7 Habits of Highly Effective People* (Simon and Schuster) 2004
- Dweck, Carol S., *Mindset: How You Can Fulfil Your Potential* (Robinson) 2012. For an example of Dweck's other work, see *Handbook of Competence and Motivation*, edited with Andrew J. Elliot (Guilford) 2005
- Kelsey, Robert, *What's Stopping You? Why Smart People Don't Always Reach Their Potential and How You Can* (Capstone) 2011

Life-roles and whole self:

- Burton, Kate, *Live Life, Love Work* (Capstone) 2010

- Buzan, Tony, 'Mind maps for self-analysis', in *The Mind Map Book: Unlock Your Creativity, Boost Your Memory, Change Your Life* (BBC Active) 2009, pp. 119 – 127.
- Ditzler, Jinny, *Your Best Year Yet: Make the Next 12 Months Your Best Ever* (Harper Element) 2006
- Mayne, Brian, *Goal Mapping: How to Turn Your Dreams into Realities* (Watkins) 2006

Mistakes and perseverance:
- Burkeman, Oliver, *Help: How to Become Slightly Happier and Get a Bit More Done* (Cannongate) 2011
- The 10,000 hour rule was made famous by Malcolm Gladwell in *Outliners: The Story of Success* (Penguin) 2009 and is based on research by psychologist Anders Ericsson. For more on Ericsson's work, see: www.psy.fsu.edu/faculty/ericsson.dp.html
- Harford, Tim, *Adapt: Why Success Always Starts with Failure* (Abacus) 2011
- Syed, Matthew, *Bounce: The Myth of Talent and the Power of Practice* (Fourth Estate) 2011

Journey-focused:
- Brach, Tara, *Radical Acceptance* (Bantam) 2004. Tara Brach's website: http://tarabrach.com
- Cameron, Julia, *The Artist's Way* (Pan) 2011 and *The Sound of Paper* (Penguin) 2006. Julia Cameron's website: http://juliacameronlive.com
- Kornfield, Jack, *After the Ecstasy, the Laundry: How the Heart Grows Wise on the Spiritual Path* (Bantam) 2001
- Shapiro, Stephen M., *Goal-Free Living: How to Have the Life You Want Now* (John Wiley) 2006. Shapiro's website: http://www.steveshapiro.com/books-and-articles/goal-free-living-book/

- See also: Burkeman, Oliver, 'The downsides of goalsetting, or why Brian Tracy makes me feel ill', (oliverburkeman.com) 2010 http://www.oliverburkeman.com/2010/12/the-downsides-of-goalsetting-or-why-brian-tracy-makes-me-feel-ill/ [Also reprinted in *Help*.]

Chapter 8: Motivation. What is it? Do you need it?
So is motivation an emotion?
- Brach, Tara, *Radical Acceptance* (Bantam) 2004. Tara Brach's website: http://tarabrach.com

Make it a habit
- Several self-help writers talk about habit. See for instance Burkeman, Oliver, 'How to Keep Functioning: Everyday Life' in *Help: How to Become Slightly Happier and Get a Bit More Done* (Cannongate) 2011, pp. 246 – 248.

Big wants and small wants
- Jinny Ditzler talks about big and little wants in *Best Year Yet* (Harper Element) 2006.

Values:
- Jinny Ditzler's *Best Year Yet* (Harper Element) 2006 is one of the best self-help books I've read on identifying your personal values. Look under question five 'What are my personal values?' You could also try:
  o Burton, Kate and Brinley Platts, *Building Self-Confidence for Dummies* (Wiley) 2005, especially chapter 5, pp. 63 - 74.
  o Burton, Kate, *Live Life, Love Work* (Capstone) 2010, pp. 146 – 148

Don't wait:

- The "don't wait until you feel like doing something" quotation is from Oliver Burkeman's blog. 'The one-sentence solution to almost all procrastination (no, really)', 5th January 2011. Available from: http://www.oliverburkeman.com/2011/01/the-one-sentence-solution-to-almost-all-procrastination-no-really/

Niggles:

- The inspiration for the practical exercise *Get rid of the niggles* was Oliver Burkeman's column 'Mild Irritation', *Guardian*, 10th March 2007 and is available from: www.guardian.co.uk/lifeandstyle/2007/mar/10/weekend.oliverburkeman

Key motivation blind spots:

- Exercise regularly and eat healthily. See: http://www.nhs.uk/Change4Life/Pages/change-for-life.aspx For a recipe book that explains how foods affect your moods, try Natalie Savona's *The Kitchen Shrink: Foods and Recipes for a Healthy Mind* (Duncan Baird) 2004.
- Creative activities: See *Creating a Life Worth Living: A Practical Course in Career Design for Aspiring Writers, Artists, Filmmakers, Musicians and Others* by Carol Lloyd (HarperCollins) 1997. For practical activities, try Bonnie Neubauer's *The Write Brain Workbook: 366 Exercises to Liberate Your Writing* (Writer's Digest) 2006 and *The Anti-Colouring Book* by Susan Striker and Edward Kimmel (Scholastic) 2007. Julia Cameron's work will also help.
- I've always wanted to: Try Jinny Ditzler's *Your Best Year Yet: Make the Next 12 Months Your Best Ever* (Harper Element) 2006.
- Quit smoking: http://smokefree.nhs.uk/

Chapter 9: Small steps to time management.
Review of time management methods:

- Allen, David, *Getting Things Done: How to Achieve Stress-free Productivity* (Piatkus) 2002. Website: http://www.davidco.com/about-gtd
- Burkeman, Oliver, 'How to Rule the Office' and 'How to Get More Done' in *Help: How to Become Slightly Happier and Get a Bit More Done*, (Cannongate), pp. 93 – 140.
- Cirillo, Francesco *The Pomodoro Technique* (Lulu.com) 2009 Available to download for free from: www.pomodorotechnique.com
- Eisenberg, Ronni, *Organise Yourself* (Piatkus) 2006
- Forster, Mark, *Do it Tomorrow and Other Secrets of Time Management* (Hodder and Stoughton) 2006 and *Get Everything Done and Still Have Time to Play* (Hodder and Stoughton) 2000. See: www.markforster.net
- Mann, Merlin, *43 Folders.* www.43folders.com

Chapter 10
Eight secrets
"The eight secrets of goal-free living" are used to structure Shapiro, Stephen M., *Goal-Free Living: How to Have the Life You Want Now* (John Wiley) 2006.

Chapter 12: Set it up, break it down, make it easy
Break it down example. Writing a novel:

- Syed, Matthew, *Bounce: The Myth of Talent and the Power of Practice* (Fourth Estate) 2011
- Ingermanson, Randy and Peter Economy *Writing Fiction For Dummies* (John Wiley) 2009

Using subheadings to break down tasks:
- Find out more about the Prince's Trust Enterprise Programme at: www.princestrust.org.uk/need_help/enterprise_programme.aspx

Essay Writing example:
- If you need help with essay writing, try a study skills book or programme. For instance, the Open University publish several books in the *Good Study Guide* series. Most of these are written by Andy Northedge with various other authors. I used the following in my example:
  - Livi-Bacci's, Massimo, *A Concise History of World Population* (Wiley-Blackwell) 2012
  - Rosenberg, Charles E., *The Cholera Years: United States in the Years 1832, 1849 and 1866* (University of Chicago) 1987

Any written piece of work:
- The Snowflake Method. See *Writing Fiction For Dummies* by Randy Ingermanson and Peter Economy (John Wiley) 2009.

Build your own house:
- *The Green Self-build Book: How to Design and Build Your Own Eco-home* by Jon Broome (Green Books) 2007.
- Alain de Botton's guide to building your own home on the channel 4 website: http://tinyurl.com/AdB-self-build-guide

Make it easy:
- For a fascinating introduction to the psychology behind 'making it easy' see 'Is the easy option simply mental laziness?' by Oliver Burkeman which appeared in the

Guardian on Saturday 20 February 2010 and is available at: www.guardian.co.uk/lifeandstyle/2010/feb/20/change-your-life-easy-option See also Burkeman, Oliver, 'The Quickest Route to Being Wrong' in *Help: How to Become Slightly Happier and Get a Bit More Done* (Cannongate) 2011, pp. 152 – 153.

Chapter 13: Make it count, keep it balanced, think whole picture
The Pomodoro Technique:
- Website: www.pomodorotechnique.com

Hierarchy of Need:
- Maslow, Abraham, 'A theory of human motivation', *Psychological Review*, No. 50, 1943, pages 370-96. For more on Maslow's Hierarchy of Needs see Atkinson, Sam et al, eds., *The Psychology Book*, (Dorling Kindersly) 2012, p. 138 – 139.

Convergent / divergent thinking:
- J.P. Guilford, 'Traits of creativity' in P.E. Vernon (ed.), *Creativity* (Penguin) 1970. For more on J.P. Guilford, see Atkinson, Sam et al, eds., *The Psychology Book*, (Dorling Kindersly) 2012, p. 305.

Chapter 15: Small adjustments
David Allen:
- Allen, David, *Getting Things Done: How to Achieve Stress-free Productivity* (Piatkus) 2002. Website: www.davidco.com/about-gtd
- There's a personal description of Allen's approach on Merline Mann's 43 folders blog: www.43folders.com/2004/09/08/getting-started-with-getting-things-done

Your filing system:

- Burkeman, Oliver, 'The Joy of Filing', in *Help: How to Become Slightly Happier and Get a Bit More Done* (Cannongate) 2011 p. 136 – 138. Reprinted from *Guardian*, Saturday 23 February 2008 and available on: www.guardian.co.uk/lifeandstyle/2008/feb/23/healthandwel lbeing.oliverburkeman/print

Chapter 16: Small Tools
Friendly magazines on I.T. published in the UK include:
- Computer Active Magazine
- Web User Magazine

For beginners' I.T. classes in your area, try:
- your local library or community centre
- your local college or adult education centre
- the Learn Direct website: www.learndirect.co.uk

Chapter 17: Small ways to keep check
Making a date with yourself:
- For lots of detail on what Julia Cameron calls 'Artists' Dates' see *The Artist's Way* (Pan) 2011.

****

About the author: Dr Louise Tondeur is a Senior Lecturer in Creative Writing at Roehampton University, specialising in Fiction. She has published two novels with Headline Review and has just finished a third. She developed the small steps method when writing her novels, completing her PhD, traveling around the world and when starting a family – without it the road to success would have been much more bumpy. She uses the small steps method with her undergraduate and postgraduate students.